Reflections ON THE
GIFTS OF
THE SPIRIT

Other books by the same author:

> *Reflections on the Baptism in the Holy Spirit*
> *Reflections on a Song of Love (1 Corinthians 13)*
> *A Trumpet Call to Women*

In course of preparation:

> *The Clash of Tongues (1 Corinthians 14)*
> *Consider Him (Twelve Qualities of Christ)*
> *Battle for the Body*
> *There Shone a Great Light (The Christmas Story)*

Reflections

ON THE

GIFTS OF THE SPIRIT

Hugh B. Black

NEW DAWN BOOKS

GREENOCK, SCOTLAND

First published 1988 by
NEW DAWN BOOKS
27 Denholm Street, Greenock PA16 8RH, Scotland

ISBN 1 870944 01 1

Unless otherwise indicated biblical quotations are
from the Revised Version

Cover photo: Craig Richardson

Production and printing in England for
NEW DAWN BOOKS
27 Denholm Street, Greenock PA16 8RH, Scotland
by Nuprint Ltd, Harpenden, Herts AL5 4SE.

Dedication

To the memory of Smith Wigglesworth in whose life and work gifts of the Spirit were so powerfully manifest. He inspired me greatly.

Acknowledgements

I am grateful to all those who continue to encourage me to write; to my daughters, Dr Alison H. Black for editorial assistance and Mrs Grace Gault for help with Greek references; to Mrs Black, Miss Jennifer Jack and Mr Alistair Duff for proof-reading and helpful advice; and to Miss Irene Morrison for laborious work in processing the various drafts of the book.

My thanks are also due to the authors and publishers whose works have been quoted, one of which I would particularly like to mention. When the corrected page proofs of this present book had already been returned to the printer, I first discovered (by the kind offices of Mr Andrew Twiddie and Mr William Kinnaird) Gordon D. Fee's *The First Epistle to the Corinthians* (Wm. B. Eerdmans Publishing Company, 1987), published in *The New International Commentary on the New Testament* series of which F. F. Bruce is the general editor. I was naturally pleased to find that much of this work supported what I had written, and I felt some of his contributions to be so valuable that I have quoted extensively in notes added at this later-than-last minute (as my longsuffering editorial assistant and printer will agree). Dr Fee's scholarship is self-evident, and the inclusion of extracts means that readers are having the benefit of the most recent research in this field.

Contents

Foreword

I have known the author for the past twenty years and have
been greatly privileged to sit many times under his ministry
and teaching. Through this, my own pastoral and itinerant
ministry in this country and overseas was brought into a
new dimension.

I know that over the years many books have been
written, many sermons preached on this theme, yet
throughout the church there is still a great deal of
ignorance, misinterpretation, and unfortunately abuse of
the gifts of the Holy Spirit. I believe, as you read prayerfully and carefully, you will find the teaching in this book
deals thoroughly and accurately with the subject, and has
been written not only from the author's knowledge of the
Scriptures but born through experience as he has taught
and ministered these truths in his own congregation and in
many other churches. Multitudes have been baptised in
the Holy Spirit, healed, and set free from demonic powers.
Many of these people are now ministering in the power
and the anointing of the Holy Spirit.

I am persuaded and confident that *Reflections on the
Gifts of the Spirit* will not only be a challenge and inspiration, but will motivate the reader to be fully prepared and
equipped 'for such a time as this.'

Rev. John Hamilton
Wilton, Yorkshire

Preface

During the last two decades there has grown a tremendous interest amongst Christians in the gifts of the Spirit and indeed a whole movement—the Charismatic movement—has derived its name from the Greek root *charisma*, which has been translated into English as 'gift.'

In earlier days the Pentecostal movement focused attention on the Baptism in the Spirit as an experience for Christians which came after conversion, and subsequently on gifts of the Spirit which were expected to be in evidence after the Baptism. The Charismatic movement, on the other hand, by virtue of its very name has focused attention very pointedly on the gifts themselves. It does, of course, recognise a fulness of the Spirit which is expected to develop in Christians after conversion. Differences of emphasis and teaching relative to the Baptism have been explored in my earlier book, *Reflections on the Baptism in the Holy Spirit,* and in this work my main purpose is to examine the gifts in some depth and to see them not only in their immediate context, but also in relation to some of the deeper fundamental teachings of the New Testament.

This book is mainly concerned with the nine gifts mentioned in 1 Corinthians 12:4–11. These, however, are not the *only* gifts of the Spirit and some allusion to others is also made.

1

Introduction

It is often wise to examine the context in which particular doctrines emerge before examining the doctrines themselves, and where the gifts of the Spirit listed in 1 Corinthians 12:4–11 are concerned, this is particularly appropriate.

Paul writes:

> Now concerning spiritual *gifts*, brethren, I would not have you ignorant. Ye know that when ye were Gentiles ye were led away unto those dumb idols, howsoever ye might be led. Wherefore I give you to understand, that no man speaking in the Spirit of God saith, Jesus is anathema; and no man can say, Jesus is Lord, but in the Holy Spirit (1 Cor 12:1–3).

The word 'gifts' included in italics does not appear in the original. The more accurate translation is 'Now concerning spirituals...'. The translators knew, however, that this would not be easily understood and they also knew that something like 'gifts' could be properly assumed. After dealing with other aspects of the background we will return to this—since the meaning of the word 'gifts' and the sense in which the word is used are of very real significance.[1]

13

In the East of Paul's day demon possession was very common, as it is in many parts of the world in our day. People acted strangely under demon influence and abnormal phenomena would frequently be witnessed. Under the power of the Holy Spirit, however, Christians also experienced and manifested supernatural phenomena. Very probably the question arose from time to time: 'How can we always be sure whether a person is acting under the power of God or under an evil power? Is there a sure test?' One might, for example, have said, 'The girl from whom Paul cast out a demon in Acts 16 was actually saying, "These men are servants of the Most High God, which proclaim unto you the way of salvation." Her words were true. How can one judge?' Paul did not deal with the words; neither, in a sense, did he deal with the girl, but with the demon which was operating through the girl, and the fact of the possession he would know by the operation of the gift of discernment. In the verses under consideration he gives general teaching which leaves the following position: the Holy Spirit glorifies Christ and the person speaking under His power recognises the Lordship of Christ. No-one speaking by the power of the Holy Spirit says, 'Jesus is anathema,' or 'Jesus is accursed.' In 1 John 4:1–2 we are told to test whether the spirits are of God:

> Beloved, believe not every spirit, but prove the spirits, whether they are of God: because many false prophets are gone out into the world. Hereby know ye the Spirit of God: every spirit which confesseth that Jesus Christ is come in the flesh is of God: and every spirit which confesseth not Jesus is not of God...

In my view, the teaching of these Scriptures is that a supernatural power operating through a person may be known by its attitude to Christ. Thus a person with a demon may with the lips profess Christ and speak well of Him, but

14

when the demon is in control an attitude of hatred to Christ will be revealed. When the Holy Spirit is in control Christ will always be glorified.

Paul goes on to indicate that there are diversities of gifts but the same Spirit (vv.4–6). There are differences of administration and diversities of operations. This is important since the person through whom the gifts operate can feel very real differences between one operation and another and might as a result be confused. Paul assures us, however, that in spite of these differences, it is all done by the same God and finally, in this matter, we learn and should particularly note that the manifestation of the Spirit is given to every man 'to profit withal' (v.7).

Now back to the thought of 'gift' and consideration of the part God plays in the operation of gifts.

I consider that the inclusion of the word *gift* has perhaps been unfortunate because of the overtones in the word as it is generally understood. I may receive the gift of a book. I may read it, or lend it, or give it away, or destroy it. It is mine to do with as I like. The right is absolute. So we tend to think that men receive gifts of the Spirit from God which become theirs to operate. This is just not so and wrong ideas on the matter have very harmful consequences. In fact, men just cannot *use* gifts of the Spirit. They may *abuse* them— but they can only really be *used in them* as God conducts the operation. In vocal gifts there may be an appearance which sometimes deceives—but in power gifts, such as healing, the reality of the operation or its sham nature quickly becomes evident in the outworking.

What then is the position? I am reminded of three verses:

All authority [power—AV] hath been given unto me in heaven and on earth. Go ye therefore, and make disciples of all the nations (Mt 28:18–19).

But ye shall receive power, when the Holy Ghost is come upon you: and ye shall be my witnesses (Acts 1:8).

For I am not ashamed of the gospel : for it is the power of God unto salvation to every one that believeth (Rom 1:16).

We see the infinite sea of Divine power above us; we see the vast area of human need around us; we realise that God wants channels through whom the power from above is to flow out to men: and for this He has chosen humans. Power comes down from above, is received by men and flows through them to a perishing world.

Similarly God wants to flow out to His Church for its upbuilding and its work. His power comes on one of His children—it may be to prophesy. The power has free course. The person prophesies. The power has found a channel. The power comes again. The channel deepens. It becomes regularly used. The person matures and onlookers say, 'So-and-so has the gift of prophesy.' But in reality So-and-so cannot prophesy. He can, however, become a channel through which it happens, by Divine power. People say he has a gift. I would say rather, 'He is used in an operation of God and never does have this under his sole control.' Perhaps I could illustrate this. In a long dry summer we may often see, in passing through hilly country, dried-up water courses. We see the uncovered stones where water once ran. We see the ravines that flowing water made. In the winter we come again. The rains have fallen: the torrents pour down the hillsides—but note, the water follows the former water courses. So it is in things of the Spirit. He comes again and again on individuals in particular ways—through tongues, prophecy, healings, miracles or whatever gift. When it happens once it is liable to go on happening. With some it may happen with one or two 'gifts'. With others all nine may be in operation. But again let me say, we cannot give ourselves these gifts, nor, being used in them, do we

16

ourselves use them. They are to be ever under His control.

We should particularly note in 1 Corinthians 12:6: 'And there are diversities of workings, but the same God, who worketh all things in all.' This does not refer merely to the giving of gift—but specifically to 'operations'.

Throughout the whole of the New Testament there run wholly consistent fundamental doctrines and to these all other teachings conform. Now one of those is the doctrine which is sometimes described as 'death to self'. Paul teaches this and basically it can be summarised as follows: a 'born again' man has two natures—the old fallen nature inherited from Adam and the new nature imparted at the New Birth which is the Christ nature. There is war between the two. If one is fed it grows; if starved it fades. The person concerned is aware of the struggle and the fact that the two cannot be reconciled. Paul recognised the wretched position in which he found himself:

> O wretched man that I am! who shall deliver me out of this body of death? I thank God through Jesus Christ our Lord (Rom 7:24–25).

Paul also gave clear teaching on how to deal with this from his own experience. He deliberately sided with the law of God working within him. He reckoned his old nature as being dead—'crucified with Christ'. Nevertheless he could say, 'I live; and yet not I, but Christ liveth in me' (Gal 2:20). Thus he went through life with a total death sentence on the old nature and opened himself for Christ to live His life through him. This is a vital doctrine which affects three areas in particular.

1. Our wills

They must be broken totally to God that His will alone may reign in us: this is difficult but essential and in a true

17

conversion the basis should normally already have been laid. The soul which finds Christ surely finds Him as Lord as well as Saviour. Paul instructs us: 'Try your own selves, whether ye be in the faith; prove your own selves.' I am often alarmed at how light Salvation is sometimes made in our day—resulting in pseudo-conversions. I am reminded of a story of the American Civil War. The South was suffering severe reverses and their emissaries met Lincoln on board a ship. A map of the country was on one of the walls and the representatives of the Confederacy pointed to it saying, 'We will yield you a line here and a boundary and a town there and there...' Lincoln listened in silence until they were done and then bringing his hand down with a bang on the table said, 'This government, the government I represent, demands all.' There was to be no divided America but rather unconditional surrender. So should it be in dealing with souls when the evangelist represents the government of God.

2. Our hearts

This can be more difficult. 'Keep thy heart,' we read, 'above all that thou guardest; for out of it are the issues of life,' and again, 'The heart is deceitful above all things, and it is desperately sick: who can know it?' The seat of the affections is desired by Christ and influenced by Satan. When the death sentence is truly applied to the heart a great stride is taken in spiritual life. I am reminded of the case of Hudson Taylor. As a young man he was in love with a young lady to whom he was about to become engaged. He was called to be a missionary in China and deeply knew his calling. He also knew that he was acceptable to the young lady but it became clear that she would not go to China. For a deeply affectionate nature the decision before him was extremely painful—but for Christ's sake he made it.

Through many trials and tribulations he went to China and ultimately founded the China Inland Mission—now renamed the Overseas Missionary Fellowship—and through his life and ministry, directly or indirectly, literally millions of Chinese will be in the Glory. I have always been deeply moved at the scene as he at last lay still in death. The Chinese requested to see the body of their Chief Pastor. One lady expressed truth beautifully as she saw that face beloved which looked so peaceful in death—'Thousands and myriads of angels have welcomed him.' A race of faith had been run. The affections of the heart had been crucified and Christ allowed to reign on that throne.

3. Our minds

I consider this to be a more difficult area than either of the other two. It is extremely difficult to crucify the mind; to refuse to argue with the Devil;[2] to refuse to follow an internal argument; to let 'the mind which was in Christ Jesus' be in us; to have our minds garrisoned of God. We do love to argue things out. We must be convinced. We must follow the dictates of reason—yes, even fallen reason—'I must understand.' Even although we realise that fallen reason has led so many different men and even learned men (maybe particularly learned men) to quite different conclusions, we still want to go this way. 'With Descartes' *Cogito, ergo sum* (I think, therefore I am) the Western world,' one said, 'was stood on its head.' It certainly proceeded to raise an altar to reason and reason is still often wrongly enthroned. I remember one of my old professors saying, 'Man is not a rational creature but a creature subject to occasional fits of rationality.' I was fascinated to discover later that when a number of British professors of philosophy met on one occasion they were amazed to discover that their philosophical outlooks differed according to their psychological types. In other words there were forces in man far more powerful than mind, which influenced mind. God deals with this level of personality and desires to control it. Readers particularly interested in this realm are referred to Appendix one.

'What then?' you say, 'should we stop thinking?' By no means!—but instead of allowing mind to be in the ascendant, let it function under God. Crucify the natural mind that the mind of Christ may be revealed. 'But,' you say, 'this is critical and maybe even dangerous. Am I to yield my mind?' Yes, it is critical and it is dangerous—to the Devil! And, yes, you are to yield your mind literally. In my view unfallen man's mind was like a radio receiver— there not to initiate thought, but to receive thought from God. With sin it swung free of God and assumed a position of dominance in man, for which it was not originally intended—with all the due consequences which resulted. With Baptism in the Spirit and the anointing of God in gifts like prophecy, the position is reversed. God dominates the thought. He controls and guides the mind and the person concerned suddenly feels that he has never had clearer perception or intelligence. He is dominated but, in being dominated, has been set free. He is functioning at his highest powers. The crucified mind has become the whole mind. The position of Eden[3] is restored. The mind is in its proper place—being used to serve, but not to rule, man.

Crucifixion in this realm is very difficult and the mind is often the last bastion to fall. Speaking of Baptism in water, I once heard David du Plessis say, 'Observe that the last part of a man to go under is his head—so it often is in the Baptism in the Spirit.' So it often is in the crucifixion of the whole man.

Frequently I used to find that just before God was about to use me my mind would be assaulted by Satan. I would be due to preach. God had given the word—the time was almost upon me when suddenly a problem would be presented. 'You must think about this now. If you don't get it solved you will be unable to settle to preach in power. Just sort it out. Hurry.' The matter could assume gigantic proportions. When I gave way to this it would have tragic consequences. I had to learn to say 'No' to the Devil; to refuse even to consider his suggestions; to remain in God. Frequently I discovered that when the occasion was over all urgency to consider the troubling matter had departed. I had been subjected to the trickery of the enemy. I learned to crucify the mind, but it was hard, and the process still has very frequently to be repeated. Moody is reputed to have said that the world had, at that time, yet to see what God could do through a man fully consecrated to Him. In my view when God finds a person totally crucified in the realm of the mind the whole world may well be affected. Some of the great saints do manifest it—but generally, I think, only intermittently. For me, this is the last bastion.

So then, it will be evident that probably all in human nature requiring crucifixion will be related to either our wills or our hearts or our minds.

In view of the fundamental nature of the doctrine of death to self, it is not surprising that in the operation of the gifts no part is left under the control of the 'old man'. All is under God, operating through the new man—but the new man is to be wholly, and to remain wholly, under the control of the Divine. Thus, in the gifts, attempt no action of your own—but be open to the action of God upon and through you. This is the way to the heights and the depths. May God be with you.

Finally, before considering the gifts individually may I give another picture to illustrate the way I view them. I do not see them in sharply defined separate categories but rather as a river. The abundant supply is God's—the river begins to run. Now in a natural river various streams flow in and to a measure retain their identities but generally interflow. The Atlantic, for example, becomes fresh for hundreds of miles where the Amazon flows into it but ultimately the waters merge. The flow of God's life comes down through men—one rivulet may be healing, another faith, another miracles. Sometimes these interflow and two or more are in action at the same time. Faith, for example, is often seen in operation with other gifts. So let the river run and be open to its flow and to its interflow that life may flow out to the Church and from the Church to the wider world of men.

Notes

[1] The phrase 'now concerning spiritual gifts' can also be translated 'now concerning spiritual people.' Gordon D. Fee takes the view that 'the better translation might be "[now about] the things of the Spirit," which would refer primarily to spiritual manifestations, from the perspective of the *Spirit's* endowment; at the same time it would point toward those who are so endowed.' See Gordon D. Fee, *The First Epistle to the Corinthians* (Wm. B. Eerdmans Publishing Company, 1987), pp. 575–76.

[2] 'But,' you say, 'should we not resist the Devil? Yes, indeed! But this does not involve arguing with him. A wise man once told me when I was in deep difficulty as a young man, 'Never argue with the Devil. He is more intelligent than you are. He will always win. Learn from Christ. In the time of temptation in the wilderness He three times refused even to consider his suggestions but answered with the Word of God alone and the Devil departed defeated.'

[3] Eden, if I may go down a side line, is a wonderful study. God made man in His own image. God is covered with light as a garment. So, I believe, was man. Why was Adam ashamed because he was naked? Probably simply because with sin, the light covering was lost and he was naked for the first time. The shame was not connected with his God-created body—but with the loss of the light covering.

2

The Gifts of
the Word of Wisdom and
the Word of Knowledge

> For to one is given through the Spirit the word of wisdom; and
> to another the word of knowledge, according to the same Spirit
> (1 Cor 12:8).

First notice that there is a very real distinction between
wisdom and knowledge. It was said of James VI of Scotland
(James I of England) that 'he was the wisest fool in
Christendom', rather misusing the word 'wise'. The truth
was that James was very knowledgeable but remarkably
unwise. This is true of many people. As we consider the
gifts of wisdom and knowledge the differences will become
very apparent.

First it should be noted that the wisdom referred to is
neither natural, nor acquired by human effort—nor does it
describe a general tendency or disposition in the person
concerned. It is a gift given through the Spirit and
specifically it is a 'word' of wisdom. This suggests supernatural revelation, which is precisely what it is. It comes
upon a person quite apart from any natural characteristic of
his own, or any humanly-induced train of thought, or any
mental process or endeavour. It cannot be commanded and

it cannot be added to. It comes from above and is complete in its revelation. It is an action of God.[1]

I always find it difficult to teach about the gift of wisdom in the abstract. People understand it much more easily as they look into examples of its occurrence and it is a primary purpose of this book to encourage people to examine the gifts in action and to help them understand something of their inner functioning.

It is not my intention to give exhaustive lists of the occurrence of any of the gifts as revealed in the Old and New Testaments but rather to take examples which will help to provide a clear understanding of what the gifts really are and of how they operate. Now some of the gifts were much in use and examples of their operations are numerous. Others, and amongst them wisdom, are less frequently mentioned but there are sufficient clear-cut examples recorded for our present purposes.

One of the best known stories about King Solomon, who was regarded as the wisest man in all the earth, seems to me to give an excellent example. Two women had children and one of the babes died. The mother of the dead child exchanged the babes, hoping that the other mother would not be able to recognise her own infant. They quarrelled and the matter was taken to Solomon. Not knowing who the real mother was he sent for a sword and proposed to kill the child and give them half each. The real mother of the child, with true mother love, could not bear such a judgement and preferred losing the child to her rival to having him killed. The other mother was prepared to accept Solomon's proposal. Solomon immediately recognised the true mother and gave her the child.

In the New Testament there are wonderful examples of the gift operating through Christ. On one occasion His enemies sought to trap Him with a question : 'Is it lawful to give tribute unto Caesar, or not?' Now they knew that if He answered, 'Yes,' they could represent Him to the people as unpatriotic, and no true leader of Israel. If, on the other hand, He said, 'No,' they could report Him to the Roman authority for sedition. There seemed to be no way out. Christ said, 'Shew me the tribute money,' and they brought Him a penny. 'Whose,' He asked, 'is this image and super-scription?' 'Caesar's,' they replied. 'Render therefore,' He said, 'unto Caesar the things that are Caesar's; and unto God the things that are God's.' He was totally out of the trap. It was a brilliant reply.

Wisdom was similarly revealed on another occasion when He asked His opponents a question. 'The baptism of John, whence was it? from heaven or from men?' Now they were on the horns of a dilemma. If they said, 'From men,' they would be in dire danger from the multitude who regarded the martyred John as a prophet. If, on the other hand, they said, 'From God,' Christ could have indicated that he, John, had testified of Him. Why therefore had they not obeyed him? They were forced to the pitiful position of saying, 'We know not.' This must have been bitterly humiliating, since they were the religious leaders of the people and on such an important matter as the recognition of a prophet, they were forced to confess ignorance. It was a public exposure.

There is a flavour about wisdom. There comes with it a feeling of well-being, a recognition that the thing revealed is right; it is good and wholesome. It will work. It meets the situation. Happy is that Church or community which has in it people with this gift. It saves many a confrontation and steers many a group past dangerous rapids. It can be used to give advice for positive action or to warn of the dangers into which wrong proposals might lead. It is an exceptionally valuable gift.

I am reminded of an incident in the life of Isobel Kuhn where I judge the gift to have been in operation. Serious obstacles lay in her pathway to the Mission Field. In an interview with Fraser of Lisuland she was told:

> I have sensed that Satan is opposing you and working through your mother and your brother. We are taught 'whom resist' when it comes to obstacles produced by the devil. I think that should be your stand. In prayer resist the devil, always remembering to be kind to those who are unconsciously his tools at the moment....
>
> Again he brooded out over the ocean thoughtfully, then added, 'I wonder if you will ever get to China. You are very young and you have great obstacles to face. Hm,' and again he lapsed into reverie. Then he began to talk as if he knew what to say: 'It is even conceivable that *after you get to Moody*, Satan will attempt to get you away. For instance, a telegram might come saying that your mother was very sick and urging you to return home immediately. Now, if that should happen, you cannot leave the moment you get the telegram. You would have to pack your trunk, for instance, and buy a ticket, and so on. Is there any Christian in Vancouver or here whom you can trust to be unprejudiced and yet godly enough to discern such a matter for you?[2]

There was, and when later an urgent telegram arrived at Moody for Isobel to go home immediately because of an injury to her father which was described as fatal, she recollected Mr Fraser's warning and prediction. She followed his instructions and in due time learned that her father was out of danger; and indeed he lived for a further twenty years.

He that is spiritual judgeth all things (1 Cor 2:15)

How did Mr Fraser know? [From whence came the wisdom?] When God's child is living close to Him and perfectly yielded to His will...it is possible for such an one to spread his mind out in the Lord's presence and catch the instruction of God especially if interceding for someone else.

By Searching, page 73.

In this case readers may feel that elements of both wisdom and knowledge were in operation.

The word of knowledge is, however, basically different from the word of wisdom. In the Old Testament we read of an incident in the life of Samuel where the gift was in operation. When he first met Saul he indicated to him that certain asses which had been lost for three days had been found and that he should no longer worry about them (1 Sam 9:20).

In the life of Christ this gift is also seen in operation. Nathaniel had been praying under a fig tree, hidden from all eyes. Christ, however, could reveal that He knew of it. The record of the incident in John 1:47–50 strongly implies that Christ's seeing of him was not natural but a revelation of God. It was enough to make Nathaniel exclaim, 'Thou art the Son of God; thou art King of Israel.'

In speaking to the woman at the well (Jn 4:16–18) Christ could tell her that she had had five husbands as He probed right to the heart of her need and confronted her with her sin. The words, 'He whom thou now hast is not thy husband,' must have fallen on her ears with disturbing power. At the end of the matter she could say to her fellow citizens, 'Come, see a man, which told me all things that ever I did' (Jn 4:29).

Again the gift was in operation when Peter revealed the duplicity of Ananias and Sapphira and their secret agreement to deceive the church (Acts 5:13). They had sold a piece of land and pretended to give the total receipt from it to the church, but had, in fact, held back part of the price. The sin was revealed by the gift of knowledge and punished with death.

In more modern times two very interesting examples of the operation of the gift are found in Demos Shakarian's book, *The Happiest People On Earth*. He tells of two incidents in Armenia before his people had received their

27

Pentecost. The operation of the gift of knowledge was used to influence a whole company in that direction. In the first case we read:

> Over the years several families living in Kara Kala had begun to accept the message of the Russian Pentecostals. Grandfather's brother-in-law, Magardich Mushegan, was one these. He received the Baptism of the Holy Spirit and on his frequent visits to the Shakarian farm would talk about the new-found joy in his life.
>
> On this particular day—May 25, 1891—Grandmother and several other women were sewing in a corner of the one-room farm house. That is, Grandmother was trying to sew, but tears kept falling on the material in her lap.
>
> Across the room, next to the window where the light was good, Magardich Mushegan sat with his Bible open on his knee, reading.
>
> Suddenly, Magardich snapped his Bible shut, got up and walked across the room. He stood in front of Grandmother, his heavy black beard bobbing up and down in his excitement.
>
> 'Goolisar,' Magardich said, '...the Lord has just spoken to me!'
>
> Grandmother's back straightened. 'Yes, Magardich?'
>
> 'He's given me a message for you,' Magardich said. 'Goolisar, exactly one year from today, you will give birth to a son.'[3]

This was exactly fulfilled, but the father 'considered himself too tough-minded to accept without reservation that he had witnessed a supernatural prophecy of the sort mentioned in the Bible. Maybe Magardich's prediction had been merely a lucky chance' (*The Happiest People on Earth*. page 17).

The second incident, however, settled matters. From time to time Russian Christians visited Armenia and in the year 1900 word came that 100 of them were on their way. Demos began to make preparations and selected his fattest steer for a special feast. The animal, however, had a defect in one eye and Demos, believing it was wrong to use this animal, hid the head beneath a pile of threshed wheat in a dark corner. The Russians arrived and just before the feast commenced, we read:

> But to Grandfather's dismay, the patriarch suddenly raised his hand—not in sign of blessing—but as a signal that everything was to stop. Giving Grandfather a strange penetrating look, the tall white-haired man walked from the table without a word.
>
> Grandfather's eyes followed the old man's every movement as the prophet strode across the yard and into the barn. After a moment he reappeared. In his hand he held the sack which Grandfatker had hidden beneath the pile of wheat.
>
> Grandfather began to shake. How could the man have known! No one had seen him. The Russians had not even reached the village when he had hidden that head...with the milk-white eye.
>
> 'Have you anything to confess, Brother Demos?' the Russian asked.
>
> 'Yes, I have,' said Grandfather, still shaking. 'But how did you know?'
>
> 'God told me,' the old man said simply. 'You still do not believe that He speaks to His people today as in the past. The Spirit gave me this word of knowledge for a special reason: that you and your family might believe. You have been resisting the power of the Spirit. Today is the day you will resist no longer.'
>
> Before his neighbours and guests that evening Grandfather confessed the deception he had attempted. With tears rolling down his face into his bristly beard, he asked their forgiveness. 'Show me,' he said to the prophet, 'how I, too, can receive the Spirit of God.'
>
> Grandfather knelt and the old Russian laid his work-gnarled hands on his head. Immediately Grandfather burst into joyous prayer in a language neither he nor anyone present could understand. The Russians called this kind of ecstatic utterance 'tongues' and regarded it as a sign that the Holy Spirit was present with the speaker. That night Grandmother, too, received this 'Baptism in the Spirit.'

The Happiest People on Earth, pages 19–20.

Some remarkable instances of the coming of supernatural knowledge took place in the Lewis Revival, associated with the name of the late Rev. Duncan Campbell. The following incidents I heard from his own lips. In a very humble thatched cottage there were two old ladies, Mary and Peggy, who really knew God. One of them indicated to the minister of the parish that he should send for Mr Campbell (whom she had never seen) to hold meetings in their church. The invitation was sent but declined owing to prior engagements. 'If, however, these should fall through,' Mr Campbell said, 'I will be willing to come.' The arrangements did fall through and Mr Campbell went. He described to me his first visit to the old ladies. 'Yes,' said the older, when he went in, 'you are God's man after all.' 'But,' he said, 'you don't know me. You've never seen me.' 'Oh yes,' she said, 'I have seen you. At a certain date the Devil tried to kill you but at three o'clock in the afternoon the precious blood of Jesus came between you and him and you were saved.' I think the colour left Mr Campbell's face. He told me that on that date at that time precisely he had been on his motor cycle between Falkirk and Glasgow and while he was overtaking a bus, a Rover car came out of a side road at sixty miles an hour, just missed him and landed over the hedge. The bus driver spoke of the 'miracle' that had happened. 'I told nobody,' said Mr Campbell. 'No,' said the old lady, 'but God told me.'

This must have been a good start to their relationship—but it certainly was not the end. The second incident I want to relate has always amused me. The Revival was under way—but there was a particular village which was untouched, and indeed opposed to the movement. One day the older lady told Mr Campbell, when he visited her, that he should go over to that particular village. He was not happy about this and told her that he had not been invited and that indeed the people over there were opposed to what was happening. A point came when he said, 'Well, we'll pray about it.' (It is amazing how often, after God tells us to do something, we compromise by saying, 'We'll pray about it.') So they prayed, or rather the old lady prayed (no inhibitions about women's ministry there) and she prayed as follows, 'Lord, I have given your servant the message you gave me but he does not appear to be willing to obey it. Lord, give this man wisdom.' I can picture Mr Campbell scratching his head as they got up from their knees and saying, 'Well, I suppose I had better go.' 'Yes,' she said, 'you had better go, and you will not be preaching for fifteen minutes before the Lord will give you seven souls.'

He went and a crowd of people had gathered in a house before he arrived. This kind of thing is difficult to explain but it does happen in revival. Once on the island of Bernera just off Lewis, for example, all were stopped in what they were doing—whether shopping, working in the fields or fishing—and were drawn as one man to the church. Revival swept that community. I have known a little of the same thing on Lewis. People can just suddenly know, without intimation, where a meeting is being held. Well, in this case the house was packed—so much so that the preacher could not get in, but preached from outside to the people inside. After about fifteen minutes one of the elders squeezed his way out and said, 'You'll have to stop and come in. There are some people in here in a terrible state.' When he got in, there were bodies prostrate on the floor and when he counted them there were exactly seven. Every one rose born again.

The secrets of the Lord are with them that fear Him. These old praying ladies had an intimacy with God of which Mr Campbell had no previous knowledge. They received supernatural knowledge of people and events as God was minded to reveal it. I myself met this kind of thing in Lewis. One of my own intimate friends, who was deeply used in the 1939 Revival, is gifted in this way. At that time the power of

God came mightily on her. She received her Baptism in the Spirit, speaking in tongues without knowing what these were. For about a fortnight she was almost constantly out of the body in what would appear to others as a trance-like condition. She was out with God. She saw the outcome of the war. She saw the dead of her own area—some going into Hell, others to Heaven. I know the house in which she was when the news of the fall of France came through. She threw up her hands and glorified God. Others wondered if they had a traitor in their midst. 'No,' she said, 'but France had to fall. There could be no victory till France fell.' She had seen it all. It is wonderful to have a friend like this but also at times disconcerting. So accurate can their knowledge be, that if something slips in my life the query may arrive, 'What happened to you a week ago last Friday? I was burdened for you.' You realise that you are known of God and of such a servant of God.

Another of my friends, nearer home, is also used in this disconcerting way. Once, many years ago, she said to me, 'I had a terrible burden for your very soul last Saturday at two o'clock.' I was very put out. At that exact time I had been in extreme danger—of which no-one in all the world knew but myself. By God's grace I had not gone down. On hearing her words, I made no comment. I did not then, nor I think even later, tell how close had been the danger. But I noted her word and was grateful. Knowledge indeed is a powerful gift.

The gift of knowledge can work too in very practical details of life—often in spheres not regarded as particularly spiritual, as with Saul and his lost asses.

I remember in my first year of university I was ill just prior to a degree examination in Political Economy. This was for me an outside subject and my main concentration had been on Philosophy and History. I had left time for Political Economy, but, being ill, was unable to study. As a result the examination came upon me when I had literally about a day and a half for preparation. This was not the result of a slipshod attitude to my work. It really was an emergency which was not of my own making. I was cast on God. Suddenly as I read, I felt drawn to particular sections of the work and had a strong impression to leave other parts alone. I obeyed the urges and questions came up in most suitable combinations. I got distinction in the examination. In fact, I was given the best mark in that subject that I ever attained. This kind of thing happened to me again and again. It never, however, gave me liberty to play the fool with regard to studying.

In later days I applied for my first Headship of a secondary school. There was much material I thought of reading, and intended to read, prior to the interview but never really settled to it. The interview was in the autumn and during the summer holidays I was deeply involved in spiritual matters and had little time to think of career. In due time the date arrived. My position did not change until about twenty-four hours before the deadline. Then God came and I felt impressed to investigate certain topics and read one particular report—the Brunton Report. This I did. The night before my interview I had a kind of preview of the proceedings and heard myself making certain responses. The hour came. I was the youngest of the candidates being interviewed and less highly promoted than the others. We were all faced with two questions and the critical one was, 'How would you take the Mount School into the Brunton era?' Imagine the impact of that question on a candidate unfamiliar with the Report. The Report had not been very long published and the other candidates were not familiar with it. By that time I could quote it and did. In fact, it was the only book I had brought with me. I was even able to criticise it. Then what I envisaged took place. I had always felt that the fact I was so deeply involved in church work might have raised a question mark in some of the inter-viewing committee—particularly if I was paid as a minister. In one of my answers I used the word 'spiritual' and that gave them an opening. They pursued the matter and I was able to reveal that I was in charge of a church—but that the position was unpaid. I almost felt a sigh of relief go round the table. I got the job. It also comes back to mind that Satan seriously assaulted me prior to this event and I believe that had he been successful I would not have got the post.

Three years later I felt I should apply for a further post. I had distinctly felt the same over my first application. I had let previous promotion pass just simply knowing that the posts and the time were not right. The time to move had come. It was my own old school and I put in my application. There were over fifty applicants and six chosen for interview. The day before appearing before the committee, I learned that one of the six was there by special invitation. He had just missed an earlier job, but had made a very deep impres-sion on the committee. Also he had excellent qualifications. This kind of information on the eve of an interview is not helpful! But God! (I once heard Dr Martyn Lloyd Jones preach a wonderful sermon on that phrase—'but God!'—I have never forgotten it.) Indeed—but God! I remember glancing at the four printed questions. I was the first inter-viewee to go in. I asked how long they wanted me to speak on each. The chairman smilingly replied, 'As long as you like—all day if you interest us.' Then I was launched and felt that God was with me. I left the interview and made my way home. I knew in my spirit that things were still in the balance. The burden was on me but there came a moment —I remember the exact spot on the road—when I knew the decision was made. The job was mine. I was so sure that when the confirming telephone call came later in the day it scarcely mattered. It was not news. That had been given me by God. How else does one explain such knowledge?

There are interesting footnotes to this story. One of the ladies on the committee asked me later, 'Did you know that you were going to get that job that day? I felt you did.' How she suspected this I do not know but I had to answer, 'Yes.' Also, when I took up the appointment four members of staff who had formerly taught me as a pupil were still there. My deputy had belted me as a first year pupil and another had been largely responsible for my going into teaching. As he said to his colleagues on my appointment, 'It shows the respect with which you should always treat your pupils— you never know! You never know!'

How does one explain the gift of knowledge? One cannot in any natural way. It is a given thing—a supernatural thing. We can only receive it and be thankful!

Increasingly in our day servants of God are used in the gift of knowledge. It frequently happens in public gatherings. Particular physical conditions are described and sometimes the persons concerned identified. Healing often results—as does conviction of sin and great encouragement depending on circumstances. The first time I ever heard it was on a tape and I really felt awe. I later witnessed it in a Kathryn Kuhlman meeting in America and was deeply impressed. Miss Kuhlman would indicate that there was someone sitting in perhaps the second back row in a particular segment of the auditorium. She would narrow the position by saying, '. . . three or four along from the end. You have been blind for years. The Hand of the Lord is on you now. Rise to your feet. He is healing you.' Very rapidly she would be dealing with another elsewhere in the gathering—cancer this time—then another and another until scores were affected. No one was allowed to move to the platform until he or she was healed. Soon the platform was besieged as great numbers responded. Their cases were open for any medical person present to investigate. It was truly impressive.

More recently the numbers used in this way have been increasing and the use of the gift is a great encouragement to the Church. A position is also created where people become more careful to avoid hypocritical living. Surely the secrets of hearts are revealed and men must declare that 'God is among you indeed'. The exposure of sin is perhaps one of the most important functions of the gift.

One of my personal friends, the Reverend John Hamilton, has been increasingly used in this ministry in public meetings in recent years. Situations and conditions are revealed to him and frequently also the identity of the people concerned. Sin is uncovered and the sense of the presence of God comes mightily upon companies. The fear of the Lord comes. The gift began to operate very quietly. On the first occasion God brought the word 'Lesbian' before him and within an hour there came a knock on his door and the person seeking help was in just such a wrong relationship. Adultery in a young newly married man was later revealed. Case followed case as the ministry developed. On one remarkable occasion he was taking a service on a Sunday morning when God brought a knowledge of 'uncleanness' before him. He wanted to deal with it but the chairman, to whom he mentioned the matter, advised against so doing. The evening service came and he felt compelled to speak of the matter publicly. By that time God had also revealed to him the identity of the person concerned. While concealing the identity, Mr Hamilton went on to speak publicly, not only of the condition, but of the fact that the person had attempted suicide that afternoon. This too he knew by revelation. Shortly after Mr Hamilton left the platform he discovered that the gentleman whom God had so clearly identified was in a desperate state of conviction. Again and again in public meetings the ministry is in operation and this kind of ministry can be very costly. It deals with wrongdoing. It is also used in giving encouragement and sometimes a knowledge of the call of God on particular lives. It is a means whereby God speaks very directly to His people. The revelation of sin is given so that people may be convicted, forgiven and set free. The revelation of call is for encouragement and edification. God is forever gracious. Again and again the call is: 'Let my people go that they may serve Me.'

There came in Mr Hamilton's life an hour which was critical and which I am sure would be of particular interest to my readers. He was in Germany at the time and after a heart-breaking day of counselling, he felt a sense of burden that he had never known before. Cases he had to deal with that day had been particularly harrowing and ultimately he cried in his spirit to God: 'Can this really be your Church?—so weak! so unclean! so divided!' Then God spoke, 'Tell my people that they have not fully realised the potential for God that is in them.' The verse 'But if the Spirit of him that raised up Jesus from the dead dwelleth in you, he that raised up Christ Jesus from the dead shall quicken also your mortal bodies through his Spirit that dwelleth in you' was quickened to him. He then heard the words: 'As the Father sent me so send I you.' Next there came a beautiful vision in which the hands of Christ were held out and Mr Hamilton saw the whole Church held in His hands. 'It was glorious,' he said. 'The hands then began to move and there was a shaking. People were thrown about everywhere. People who were on the mission field, whom God had never sent, came home again. People who were at home, who should have been on the field, went out. When the hands became still every Christian was in his or her right place. Not one was out of place.' (Will it not take a worldwide revival of phenomenal power to accomplish this—and does this vision not give ground for hope?). 'Then,' said Mr Hamilton, 'as I waited before God I became aware that there was something new to happen in my own experience.

37

Suddenly I heard the cry of His people and I don't think I ever heard a sound or a cry like it in my life. Then God spoke: "Have you heard this cry?" "Yes, I have heard it." "What will you do about such a cry?" "Lord, there is nothing I can do about such a cry." "That is right. Rise up on your feet and stand and go." The time was about three o'clock in the morning and Mr Hamilton went into another apartment where a number of people were praying. As he went through the doors one of the group was prophesying in German (which Mr Hamilton could not understand). Immediately afterwards he asked about what had been said and it fitted his situation exactly. 'I have surely seen the affliction of my people...and have heard their groaning...and I am come down to deliver them (Acts 7:34; cf. Ex 3:7). Come now, I will send you.' 'I knew in that moment,' said Mr Hamilton, 'that God was saying this in my spirit. Many times since then I hear that cry in meetings and when I hear it, people are healed just where they sit. One of the most important things associated with the experience of that night is the setting of people free from bondage. When I visit a company for the first time I always speak of this experience.'

In our own fellowship the gift has been in operation for a long time. I have known danger being discerned and the people concerned identified, long before there was a ripple on the waters. The knowledge enabled the leadership to give particular vigilance to the danger as it developed. They had a spiritual knowledge of its source and had been prepared to handle it.

On one particular occasion I met a young man at our church door and had a most amazing reaction to him. Never, I think, did I feel such revulsion to any individual. He was unknown to me but the reaction was extreme. A short time passed and I arrived one Sunday night for the evening service to be informed that this young man had arrived in the afternoon and mixed with our young people. To one of them he described quite accurately the young lady in whom he was interested. The other was shocked. He had indicated nothing to the young lady or anyone else. He felt his privacy had been painfully invaded. As it happened the newcomer turned out to be one of the most clairvoyant people I have ever met—the illegitimate son of a medium. I went into the pulpit that night, as you may imagine, with my own thoughts and at the end of the service requested, or perhaps I should say ordered, the young man to come with me to the vestry. There battle commenced. Later he confessed that he tried and failed to dominate me. Suddenly he dropped to the floor and his head went down. Seemingly he could not raise it again. God was with me.

Eventually the lad professed Salvation and I believe made a genuine effort. He was, however, grievously tormented by evil powers and at that time there was little experience of exorcism amongst us. The young man was unemployed and not in very good health and asked to be allowed to come into the church in daytime and work around it. This was quite acceptable and a considerable period passed. Suddenly one day a word of knowledge came to one of the leaders and I was asked if the lad had a key to the church. 'Yes,' I said, explaining the position. 'Well, you should get the key back. There is danger threatening.' My position was awkward. I said, 'Well, you know, he has behaved very well. I really can't fault him since I let him have the use of the church.' 'That may be,' was the reply 'but I warn you—get the key back.' I went to see the lad and said, 'Look, you are not under criticism but there is a cloud over you at the moment and while it remains I want the key of the church.' He quite happily accepted this and showed no ill-will. A few weeks passed and his attendance dropped off. Then suddenly one night a lady arrived asking if this young man attended the church. 'Well,' I said, 'he did but lately he has dropped off.'

She went on to reveal homosexual offences involving him— there was real trouble—and, had there been no warning, the offences might well have occurred right in the church building. Was I grateful for revelation and knowledge! Through the years it has been constantly in operation in this kind of way.

Notes

[1] Writing on the word (or message) of wisdom and the word (or message) of knowledge, Fee makes the following points: 'The phrase means either "a message/utterance full of wisdom" or "an utterance characterized by wisdom".' It has nothing to do with 'the ability to give wise advice'. The '"utterance of wisdom" comes "through the Spirit".' (Fee, *First Epistle to the Corinthians*, p.592.) Of the second he writes, 'Most likely... it is a "spiritual utterance" of some revelatory kind' (*ibid.*, p.593). 'Some have suggested that Paul here has in mind a supernatural endowment of knowledge, factual information that could not otherwise have been known without the Spirit's aid, such as frequently occurs in the prophetic tradition... others see it as referring to something more akin to inspired preaching, perhaps related to receiving Christian insight into the meaning of Scripture' (*ibid.*, pp.592–93). Fee expresses surprise that Donald Gee shared the latter view. Gee maintained that this gift need not necessarily be regarded as a supernatural manifestation. But it should be remembered that the occurrence of the gift has become very widespread since Gee's day and was not much manifest in Britain then. Gee's view of the word of wisdom was also more general than that outlined above, although he did concede the possibility of revelation on the basis of the word of Jesus to his disciples in Luke 21:15 (Fee, p.592).

[2] Isobel Kuhn, *By Searching* (China Inland Mission, 1957), pp. 58–59.

[3] Demos Shakarian, as told to John and Elizabeth Sherrill, *The Happiest People on Earth* (Hodder and Stoughton, 1977), p. 16.

3

The Gift of Faith

PART 1
*A general discourse on faith (and prayer)
with personal reminiscences*

To another faith, in the same Spirit (1 Cor 12:9).

I remember in earlier days, as a teacher of history, I came on areas in which I was particularly interested and which I taught enthusiastically. There were, however, other areas, for example social history (then coming into vogue), which I found less engaging and which I probably taught less well. I find a similar tendency in writing a book. In covering the general subject particular points come up which require to be dealt with but which may not be of overriding interest to me. On the other hand, there are areas which are of very particular concern. For most of a life-time faith has been in this category.

There are two themes which are almost constantly on the lips of Christians: faith and prayer. But despite this, I have found that there really is profound ignorance on both subjects. Prayers are offered regularly with little or no expectation of fulfilment. There are many who, on being pressed, will testify that they have never really known a definite answer to prayer. Prayer meetings become 'done things' and the saying of prayers seems to become an end in itself. I am reminded of Finney who said with reference to Christian prayer meetings he attended prior to his conversion:

> I was particularly struck with the fact that the prayers that I had listened to, from week to week, were not, that I could see, answered. Indeed, I understood from their utterances in prayer, and from other remarks in their meetings, that those who offered them did not regard them as answered.
>
> When I read my Bible I learned what Christ had said in regard to prayer, and answers to prayer. He had said, 'Ask, and you shall receive, seek and you shall find, knock and it shall be opened unto you. For every one that asketh receiveth, and he that seeketh findeth, and to him that knocketh it shall be opened.' I read also what Christ affirms, that God is more willing to give his Holy Spirit to them that ask him, than earthly parents are to give good gifts to their children. I heard them pray continually for the outpouring of the Holy Spirit, and as often confess that they did not receive what they asked for.
>
> They exhorted each other to wake up and be engaged, and to pray earnestly for a revival of religion, asserting that if they did their duty, prayed for the outpouring of the spirit, and were in earnest, the spirit of God would be poured out, that they would have a revival of religion, and that the impenitent would be converted. But in their prayer and conference meetings they would continually confess, substantially, that they were making no progress in securing a revival of religion.
>
> This inconsistency, the fact that they prayed so much and were not answered, was a stumbling-block to me. I knew not what to make of it. It was a question in my mind whether I was to understand that these persons were not truly Christians, and therefore did not prevail with God, or did I misunderstand the promises and teachings of the Bible on this subject, or was I to conclude that the Bible was not true? Here was something inexplicable to me; and it seemed, at one time, that it would almost drive me into scepticism. It seemed to me that the teachings of the Bible did not at all accord with the facts which were before my eyes.

On one occasion, when I was in one of the prayer-meetings, I was asked if I did not desire that they should pray for me. I told them, no; because I did not see that God answered their prayers. I said, 'I suppose I need to be prayed for, for I am conscious that I am a sinner; but I do not see that it will do any good for you to pray for me; for you are continually asking, but you do not receive. You have been praying for a revival of religion ever since I have been in Adams, and yet you have it not. You have been praying for the Holy Spirit to descend upon yourselves, and yet complaining of your leanness... You have prayed enough since I have attended these meetings to have prayed the devil out of Adams, if there is any virtue in your prayers. But here you are praying on, and complaining still.' I was quite in earnest in what I said, and not a little irritable, I think, in consequence of my being brought so continually face to face with religious truth; which was a new state of things to me.

But on farther reading of my Bible, it struck me that the reason why their prayers were not answered, was because they did not comply with the revealed conditions upon which God had promised to answer prayer...[1]

Now this presents a very different picture of prayer from that given in the Bible. There it is seen as a vital spiritual operation, a means of obeying God and receiving from Him that which He desires to give, a wholly meaningful experience. It is closely linked with faith and faith is considered to be of absolutely critical importance. Now again faith is much misunderstood. The word is bandied around and a general view taken that if we only believe we will receive what we ask for. So, I may query; 'What have you received along this line?' 'Well, not anything, really.' 'Why not?' 'Well, maybe it is because my faith is weak.' 'Tell me, what do you think faith is?' 'Just believing that you'll get what you ask for,' etc. etc. Quickly one realises that this is highly unsatisfactory and just does not work.

So much then for the unreal—what of the real? My

interest in this field started in very early days. I owe much to Hudson Taylor and in this realm I noted his attitude: either the promises of the Bible work or they do not work. They are either true or untrue—but since they are the promises of God they must be true and if they do not work for me then there must be something wrong with me and I must discover what it is and sort it. He got down to fundamental reality and discovered deep principles of faith and prayer which are of vital importance. The tremendous work accomplished by the China Inland Mission may be largely seen as the outworking of these principles. A very able leader, Hudson Taylor refused to rely on his own ability in directing the Mission. God's work, he reasoned, should be done in God's way. When new missionaries arrived he did not decide where to send them, to reason which area was most in need, but rather sought God for guidance and then obeyed His voice. In answer to believing prayer literally thousands of missionaries went to China and were fully supported without any appeal for money from any other than God. Millions of pounds came in and millions of souls found Christ. Similarly C. T. Studd founded the Worldwide Evangelization Crusade. The same principles were employed with God-glorifying results. In a different type of work George Müller also walked with God in faith. Without any appeal to men he founded the Bristol Orphanages and received the means to support an incredible number of orphans. The work was wholly based on faith in God. He received and obeyed his call and God met all needs gloriously.

First, it is wise to take into account all the teaching of the Bible on the subject of faith, not just isolated verses. When the teaching is collated it becomes clear that the promise that we will receive what we ask for really means that we will be walking close enough to God to hear His voice, that He will convey His desire to us and that we will make His desire ours and we will make request according to His will. We will have faith (which itself is God-given) to believe that the thing will be received. In short, there is an operation of God through man which is entirely effective. Verses which should be particularly taken into account are:

> Ask, and it shall be given you; seek and ye shall find; knock, and it shall be opened unto you: for everyone that asketh receiveth; and he that seeketh findeth; and to him that knocketh it shall be opened (Mt 7:7–8).

> If ye have faith as a grain of mustard seed, ye shall say unto this mountain, Remove hence to yonder place; and it shall remove; and nothing shall be impossible unto you (Mt 17:20).

> And all things, whatsoever ye shall ask in prayer, believing, ye shall receive (Mt 21:22).

> If ye abide in me, and my words abide in you, ask whatsoever ye will, and it shall be done unto you (Jn 15:7).

> Verily, verily, I say unto you, If ye shall ask anything of the Father, he will give it you in my name. Hitherto have ye asked nothing in my name: ask, and ye shall receive, that your joy may be fulfilled (Jn 16:23–24).

> Ye ask, and receive not, because ye ask amiss, that ye may spend it in your pleasures (Jas 4:3).

> And this is the boldness which we have toward him, that, if we ask anything according to his will, he heareth us: and if we know that he heareth us whatsoever we ask, we know that we have the petitions which we have asked of him (1 Jn 5:14).

This really leaves no room for human initiative at all. This is always the way with God—and frequently man resents it. The flesh wishes to glory in its accomplishments. We may want to be great men of faith and do great things. But what did the giants do? They walked with God; they heard His voice; they obeyed His commands; they believed

His promises and there was a fulfilment of the things spoken. Take Abraham, for example. He received the promise of a land—he found it. He was a 'friend of God'. God spoke to him again and again. God promised him Isaac in impossible circumstances. He simply believed God and Isaac was born. He was told to sacrifice Isaac and again he obeyed. He told his servants as he and Isaac parted from them on their way to Mount Moriah, 'I and the lad will go yonder and worship, and come again to you.' He left them fully intending to obey God and take the life of his son, and he believed that he and his son would come back to them again. He knew that God had promised to bless all nations through the seed of Isaac and so he was fully convinced that God would raise Isaac, if necessary, from the dead. This was faith and it pleased God and God honoured it. Abraham became, indeed, a pioneer of the spiritual way, and the principles of faith that were evident in his life can be very instructive for us. Hudson Taylor discovered them, George Müller of Bristol and C. T. Studd all entered into their richness, with results for the work of God which are far beyond our knowledge.

My own early quest was interesting and perhaps not untypical. At first I suppose I thought God could be manipulated and I certainly found that others did. I clearly remember, as a young boy, praying, 'O God please give me... (something much too embarrassing to mention) if it be Thy will and if it is not Thy will, please make it Thy will for Christ's sake, Amen.' This prayer was totally serious and honest and there was no intended irreverence in it. It was based on my idea of the omnipotence of God. God could do anything. Observe the preposterous nature of my attitude. God was to rearrange His whole universe for me. He was to alter His will to conform to my will. I was a child and I was without hypocrisy. So often I come on the same attitude in adults—but usually covered with a cloak of self-deception. They are not really anxious to know what

God wants. They want Him to do what they want. I remember, again from early days, that a young lady used to come to me for help. I was a zealous young Christian, keen to lead others to Christ. Her problem was the fact that she had been taught that as a Christian she ought not to marry an unbeliever and there was a distinct shortage of suitable male believers around. One by one she brought the boys. She wanted me to win them for Christ—no doubt for their sakes and Christ's but also, and I suspect largely, for her own sake! Somehow it did not work. There might be an occasional profession. In these days I suspect it might have seemed easier for some folks to 'give in' than endure more of my arguments! Such decisions were unreal and in time I did learn! I remember that in the midst of all this the lady asked me how to get guidance. There she was, not really looking for guidance—but wanting God to rubber stamp her own arrangements! And this kind of thing is by no means uncommon amongst adult Christians who ought to know better.

Having explored some of the negative points related to prayer perhaps I should add a more positive note. In my opinion faith and prayer are two of the most potent weapons in a Christian's armoury. In true prayer a burden comes from God. The person receiving it may find that there is almost nothing he wants to do but bear it. He may carry it for hours, or days, or months, or over lengthier periods. He holds the matter constantly before God in his spirit. Prayer in connection with the burden may be voiceless or vocal. It can be carried in his aloneness or in company with others. As he prevails the burden passes away and he knows he is through to God on the matter and will inevitably receive what he has asked. He may, of course, equally know that with the passing of the burden, a life for whom God has been striving has resisted beyond a critical point and God is speaking no more. The person praying, however, has been faithful to God and has fulfilled his duty.

I remember once being deeply burdened for a pupil who had come to a crisis point in life. Through a sleepless night I strove for the soul. With the coming of dawn the burden passed and I knew that the wrong decision was sealed. These things are very real and can be very sad.

In my early Christian experience I knew nothing of intercessory prayer and even after Pentecostal experience and the opening of a real work for God, I still knew nothing of prayer burden, and said as much with reference to the on-going work of which I was the leader. I was told sharply, '*You* may have no burden but others have.' I noted this and waited with patience—realising that God divides the functions within the Body. In due time prayer burdens began to be given, although I have never felt this to be my own main ministry. I do, however, consider prayer to be one of the most vital functions in the Church. It is in the realm of prayer that Satan is defeated and the work of God accomplished. Frequently the outward side of Christian victory which men see is really the outworking of what is accomplished in the prayer chamber. If you have been given this ministry value it very highly. It is one of the most important any man or woman can receive. It works in conjunction with its sister, faith, and Paul could say that through faith mighty men of old 'subdued kingdoms, wrought righteousness, obtained promises, stopped the mouth of lions, quenched the power of fire, escaped the edge of the sword...' (Heb 11:34).

For readers interested in pursuing this theme I would recommend the writings of C. G. Finney on the subject; the biographies of Rees Howells and Praying Hyde; and the diaries of David Brainerd. The ministry of men of this kind was really phenomenal and can be a great encouragement to others to walk the same pathway.

The name of Praying Hyde reminds me of another aspect

I should perhaps mention in relation to prayer. It is very wrong to think of prayer as a cold unemotional exercise. It is based on love — warm passionate love — the love of Christ Himself. I can never forget the impact on me of the teaching of Praying Hyde. He himself lived what was virtually a life of prayer and was deeply moved with compassion. He believed and taught that Christ's sufferings did not end at Calvary but that He goes on suffering — still touched with the feeling of our infirmities — still vitally concerned with the death of the lost and with the sins of the Church. He viewed Him as still walking the Calvary road for men. If this is true it makes a difference and I am increasingly convinced it is true. For an up-to-date personal experience of the revelation of the compassion of Christ see Appendix two.

In my view, in eternity there will be vast surprises. Many who are now first may be last and many now unknown will shine as the stars for ever. In the ranks of the latter I expect praying saints to be very numerous. It is a glorious ministry. Seek it.

Fortunately, in my early days, I came on the biographies of Hudson Taylor, George Müller and C. T. Studd. I came in contact with Norman Grubb and listened with fascination to his teaching on 'death to self' and faith. The lines were being laid and convictions which have endured for a lifetime took root.

This was fortunate because, when the work with which I am associated was in what I may describe as its embryonic stage, a vital issue arose. There were five of us meeting simply to seek God. We wanted an old-time depth of religion. We were interested in holiness, revival, Pentecost. We believed that conviction of sin preceded an awakening. There was no thought of starting a new work or church. It was God Himself we sought. He moved very mightily with us. One member was particularly gifted in leading the rest of us into the sanctuary and revealing Christ. Through her, gifts were distributed and on one occasion I was so identified in prophecy that there was no doubt of the personal nature of the message. As the word was given a spiritual mantle, like a cloak, fell on me, covering head and shoulders, and words, unexpected words, were spoken, which were later to be remarkably fulfilled. Commission was given and prediction made. To my intense surprise I found fear, of which I had previously had no knowledge, being rooted out of me. I left that house with a boldness to preach the gospel I had never previously known, and there were wonderful consequences. In due time and for years, an open-air witness was set up which regularly drew crowds, hundreds strong, to hear the gospel and there were many professions of Salvation. The meetings started at 11.00 pm on Saturdays and 10.00 pm on Sundays and for years no rain, or at least not enough rain to stop an outdoor meeting, fell on Greenock at these times—and some would say, 'That was itself a miracle!'

Well, into this little group came an early note of discord and it was in relation to faith. Under discussion was James 5:14–15 and specifically what was implied in the words 'the prayer of faith shall save him that is sick.' Three of the group maintained that these words gave us a right to demand healing, that the responsibility for the faith was ours and we should exercise it. Two of us disagreed. I took the view that faith came from God and unless He gave it in each case there would be no healing. The argument ultimately came down to the question of whether in this matter the initiative came from God or from the people praying. 'The warrant,' the others said, 'is already given in this word. All you have to do is act on it, believe it.' 'The position is laid down in the Word,' I agreed, 'but the acting on it must be under God and not on our own efforts.' The argument spread beyond prayer for the sick, to the general field of faith and prayer.

I tend to be quite a pragmatic person and while being

50

deeply interested in mystical (Christian) things, keep my feet fairly firmly on the ground. Like Hudson Taylor I believed that things either worked or they did not and that we ought to come to terms with reality and truth. 'Does this that you teach work or does it not? If it works surely you are responsible to employ it. Will you pray for the salvation of twenty souls on Sunday night...or forty...or whatever number? You believe you will get what you ask for and that believing is something you can do—then why not do it? Show me the evidence—' 'Ah, but...' 'No "Ah, buts". Friends, it works or it does not!' It did not work. In the case of this little group it might have ended in tragedy—but God was gracious. The sister of one of the members was dying with cancer. The assertion was made that she would recover; the demand was made on God that it would be so. I had recently been baptised in the Spirit and, as was so common in these days, with others I laid hands on her on one occasion to pray for her healing. I felt as though the power of God drained out of my body. From this I learned to be careful in the matter of laying on of hands for healing. In spite of all human action the lady died—but so strong was the drive in others that there was talk of seeking her resurrection from the dead. Now all this was based—not on the Word of God—but on man trying to exercise faith. Such an experience could shipwreck young believers. To my mind the receiving of the *rhēma*—the particular word of God—is of vital importance and should be more widely taught. I would refer readers to *The Fourth Dimension* by Paul Y. Cho in this connection. I should perhaps refer to one more personal experience by way of illustration before coming directly to the particular gift of faith.

After the revival in the Hebrides with which the late Duncan Campbell was associated I received a letter from a friend who was at that time on the Island of Lewis. As I read the letter I felt strongly that, under God, I could put a matter right to which the letter referred and, since it was the summer break from teaching, I was free to go. This I did. Within about twenty-four hours of being on the island, three of us found ourselves on the little peninsula on which the castle stands. We had sat down on a grassy knoll. The other two chatted away, when suddenly I felt God draw near and begin to speak to me. Now I am not using metaphoric language. I literally mean the words, 'He began to speak to me'. The whole experience was remarkable and indeed life-changing. I had been through a time of great spiritual darkness and discouragement was heavy upon me. I had come to Lewis to sort a particular situation and hopefully to carry the teaching of Pentecost to as many as would hear the message. As I sat on that mound that day the difficulty of my position was strongly upon me. I had no real faith. As I was reviewing what I had been through and the position in which I found myself suddenly God said, 'Do you believe that in spite of all these things I can do this through you?' And to my shocked surprise my spirit answered, 'No.' First, I was shocked at saying 'no' to God—I had never done it before; and secondly, I was shocked to find that my spirit could answer without my mind being consulted. I never knew my spirit could answer at all. It had never happened before. With my mind I might have said, 'Yes,' because I knew I was speaking to God— but it would have been a lie. The response of my spirit was the truth. I did not believe God could do it through me and I was deeply shocked. God was exceedingly gracious. He spoke no chiding word but He began to point me to the life of Abraham. Gently He took me through that life and showed me the impossibility of the situation Abraham faced. He was to kill his only son, the son miraculously born, and still believe that God would make of that son a great nation and use his seed in the blessing of all mankind. In spite of all the painful appearances Abraham believed

God and it was reckoned to him for righteousness. Again the voice came, 'In spite of all these things do you believe that I can do this work through you?' And again it was my spirit which responded and this time the answer was, 'Yes.' Immediately I entered the realm of the miraculous. The power of God was all around. We rose; the others had fallen silent. I said no word. One remarked, 'You know, I could have burst out in tongues as we sat back there!' The whole atmosphere had become charged with the power of God. On this same occasion God made it clear to me that I must lean on no denomination or man in my work for Him. I must lean on Himself alone. And this He has never changed.

What was the effect? A burden of prayer came on me. The situation I had come to sort was sorted. Immediately the island began to open up and house meetings were arranged in many parts. I cannot in this book go into the full story of my experiences on Lewis. I may one day do this in a separate work. Suffice, at the moment, to say that many people were mightily baptised in the Spirit; I knew and experienced angelic ministry and indeed my own ministry was revolutionised.

This, to my mind, is how faith actually works. God speaks. His servant hears. The servant believes and acts on the belief. The thing promised is fulfilled. The action begins in God and continues in God and the results are God's. The self is ever in the position of death and God is glorified as He operates upon and through the new Christ-nature which He has given His children.

I was fortunate in having a background deeply prepared in earlier years so far as my understanding of the theory of faith was concerned—but I was to find that there was a difference between knowing the doctrine theoretically and actually experiencing it in action. In due time I was to find faith operate not only in things obviously spiritual such as Salvation, healing, exorcism and Baptism in the Spirit but also in the world of brick and mortar. Without ever having any rich members in our congregations, He has, over the last thirty years, miraculously guided and opened doors through faith until today this movement which He has built has property, free of debt, the value of which for insurance purposes could be fairly estimated at over a million pounds. Faith really does work. Position after position was taken in this way. What God initiated God fulfilled. When I tried to hurry things on and increase our funds my way it failed dismally. God was not minded to have human means steal His glory. I am reminded of the view of Hudson Taylor that God's work done in God's way never failed to have God's supply. From the life of George Müller, I would like to relate a further incident which illustrates faith in action.

On one occasion he was due to preach in America and he found himself delayed through fog as he crossed the Atlantic. Müller had no doubt of God's will with regard to the preaching engagement but time began to press. The ship's captain was a Christian and the two men went to his cabin to pray at, I think, Müller's suggestion. From the cabin the weather conditions could not be observed. The captain was of the opinion that Müller could not arrive on time. Müller prayed and by faith accepted the removal of the fog. The captain was about to pray when Müller stopped him saying, 'Don't you pray. In the first place you don't believe that God will move the fog and in the second place there is no need, since He has already done so.' They went on deck. The fog was gone. Müller fulfilled his engagement. You see, Müller walked sufficiently close to God to hear His voice. He knew he should accept the appointment. He knew God makes no mistakes. He believed he would be on time. He would hear the whisper in the cabin that the fog was gone. It would not be difficult for him to believe it. He lived that way.

Now what should people do who have not found this

way? Should they go on for ever hoping and trying to work up their believing? By no means! This kind of thing kills real faith and leads to the position in which a boy once found himself on being asked to define faith: 'It is,' he said, 'believing something you know isn't true.' Unanswered prayer and hopeless attempts in the realm of faith do not increase but deeply diminish faith. It is often so much easier to pray for healing or the Baptism in the Spirit for people who have never previously sought such ministry than it is to pray for folks who have gone forward unsuccessfully in numerous services. No, do not continue on a wrong way and when you make a mistake on a matter of guidance, do not go on as though nothing has happened. Investigate and find out what has gone wrong. Learn for the future. A lady once wrote to me indicating that God had called her to South Africa and she was going out on faith. I was unhappy with her spiritual condition at the time and did not really believe that this was a call from God. I remember writing back and telling her that having made her declaration, if it did not materialise, she should not just dismiss the incident as though it was of no importance—but, as a result of it, examine her whole position with reference to guidance. Too often we pass on as though nothing had happened. It reminds me of an embarrassing incident a number of years ago.

Rain was falling very heavily on Greenock as it frequently does. I found myself in a shop, having to cross a road junction diagonally to get to my next call. The rain refused to slacken and the shop girl loaned me her umbrella. It was a very bright red, I remember. Nothing daunted, I put it up and dashed across the street. On the other side the camber of the road was quite steep and I stumbled, measuring my length in the gutter which by this time was running deep with water. School children were milling past just at the critical moment and who amongst us is unable to enjoy the misfortunes of a man in the gutter—particularly a man with a lady's red umbrella? It was a painful experience but I got up as though nothing had happened to me—as though I was quite unhurt and not at all soaking wet, and proceeded at as dignified a pace as I could muster to my next port of call. What had happened to that man in the gutter had nothing to do with me! I think I did, however, take the red umbrella down. Is it not so often like this in spiritual things? We pass on as though the misfortune had not occurred—instead of taking stock and learning from the experience. If you have been on the wrong road on this matter—open your mind, there awaits you a wonderful world of adventure and reality in the kingdom of God.

There is one further incident I would like to relate. When Rees Howells was receiving medical training prior to going to Africa (to conduct a revival which God had promised would take place and in which ten thousand souls would believe) he was living by faith. One of his fellow students, who had no experience of this way of life but was interested, was given help by Rees Howells. The incident is rather amusing.

On one occasion he [Rees Howells] only had a few days in which to get £20. This was for Mrs Howells's admission to a maternity course in the City Road Hospital, for which she was coming down to London. There was another student, a Cambridge graduate, who had been saying openly that he had never prayed a prayer that had brought a direct, definite answer. So Mr Howells invited him to join in this prayer for £20. He had never heard of praying for money like that and expecting it to come. They were to pray for two hours one afternoon, each in his own room. The young man was exhausted at the end of it! He had never known time go so slowly; he said the two hours were like two months! Mr Howells did not pray through in the afternoon, so suggested that they should go back for a further two hours in the evening. 'What!' exclaimed his friend, 'four months' hard labour for £20!' However, he agreed to try again if Mr Howells thought he could be of any help. Before the end of this second period of prayer, Mr Howells went to his room, and said, 'You don't need to pray any more, I am through.' 'Have you got the money?' he said, 'No, but I have got the faith, and the money will come.' Late that night they were taking a walk together, when this student suddenly stopped, leant against a fence and roared with laughter. 'What are you laughing at?' Mr Howells asked. 'I was just thinking of the chap who will have to give that £20.' He had seen it. Two days later Mr Howells received two £10 notes. What a blessing it was when he went to his friend's room and held them up for him to see![2]

You will not find the walk of faith necessarily easy. As we die to ourselves it becomes easier—but tests can be severe and Satan greatly opposes progress. A man of faith constitutes a real danger for him. This is a realm in which real battles are lost or won and it should receive the serious attention of all who aim to go forward in God. To many a man of God it has become, with prayer, a dominating concern.

Notes

[1] Charles G. Finney, *An Autobiography* [originally *Memoirs of Charles G. Finney*] (Fleming H. Revell Company, 1908), pp.9–11.

[2] Norman P. Grubb, *Rees Howells Intercessor* (Lutterworth Press, 1973), pp.159–160.

4

The Gift of Faith

God has given a measure of faith to all men. Even in things material we are constantly exercising faith. We board a train; we trust the driver. We take our car; we trust others to observe the rules of the road and so it goes on. In the spiritual world we cannot begin without faith. The starting point itself—the New Birth—is received through faith. Now there is a difference between what I would call general faith and the gift of faith, and when people speak of faith it is usually general faith to which they are referring, and views about this, as we have seen, can be very vague and sometimes positively mistaken. I think it might help us to analyse what faith really is. The synonym which springs immediately to my mind is 'trust'. When I say, 'I have faith in God,' I am saying, 'I trust God.' Now people sometimes almost feel virtuous and humble when they say, 'You know, brother, my faith is sometimes very weak.' Have you ever analysed what such a person is actually saying (and many of us do say just such things)? Let me give you an illustration. I have a daughter in America. Suppose she comes home on vacation and as she is about to leave us again I say, 'Well Alison, I know you have missed the family badly over these last few years. I'll try to make things easier for you. I'll send you a tape every week.' Shortly afterwards I overhear Alison speaking to her sister Mary saying, 'You know, Dad has promised to send me a tape every week but I don't believe he'll do it. I just don't trust him.' This would just about break my heart. You see I was brought up to be careful about making promises and I believe in fulfilling them when they are made, and I do not deal with my daughters carelessly in such matters. What Alison said would go beyond not believing my promise. It would reflect on my character. She would judge that I was a person in whom she could not place trust. Such a wound would remain with me for a lifetime! This, friends, is the kind of thing we do with God when we say we have no faith. It is a reflection not only on what God says but on what God is—on His very character. Could I underline this. We tend in natural things to believe what people say on the ground of their character and trustworthiness, and for us to say to a friend, 'I don't believe you. I don't trust you,' is highly insulting. Why then insult God? We may not do it with impunity. As we know God our faith develops, for He is forever trustworthy and never lets his children down.

Now the gift of faith is the sudden coming of a super-natural believing for something or someone in particular circumstances.[1] The Bible is full of examples. We have witnessed it in the life of Abraham. It worked powerfully in Moses as plague upon plague came on Egypt. It was seen in Samuel when he anointed David to be king. It was evident in the life of Elijah when he prayed and for three years no rain fell and when he prayed again the rain came. It was also powerfully witnessed when he discomfited the priests of Baal on Mount Carmel. Perhaps rather than go through a long list of cases I should refer readers to Hebrews chapter 11 where the writer refers to great men and women of faith who had lived in Old Testament days. Again and again in their lives the gift was in operation.

In the life of Christ and the apostles again there are examples too numerous to mention. It should be observed, however, that frequently the gift operated in conjunction with another gift, or with other gifts. For example, when Christ healed the sick, faith and healing were both in operation. When He walked on the water, faith and miracle came together, as they did when He multiplied the loaves and fishes and raised the dead. Faith and healing again operated together when Peter prayed for the lame man at the gate of the Temple. Faith and discernment were in operation when Paul exorcised the girl with the spirit of divination.

In my view faith is involved when any gift of the Spirit is in operation. As we deepen in a gift, faith becomes almost automatic and may escape our notice. For example, when a person first prophesies, real faith is often essential. After being frequently used in the gift, the person may enter an abiding place of faith on the matter and scarcely be conscious of a particular gift of faith as he prophesies—but the gift, in fact, is there.

I have noticed in ministering to people for the Baptism in the Spirit, or for healing or exorcism, that again and again the coming of particular faith is vital. There are times when there comes clear knowledge of the will of God and, with that knowledge, faith is given. When the faith is given one can be sure of the outcome. There comes with the gift the dominance of God and one can enter a realm where, under God, one can command, and the command is obeyed. The person is baptised, or healed, or delivered as the case may be. Smith Wigglesworth used to say that there were times when he got to the end of his own faith and there entered into him the faith of the Son of God. This, I feel, happens when the gift of faith is given. It is a gloriously complete thing. I have found this gift operate in the three realms I have indicated. It also operates in preaching. God gives a word and there is faith to believe it is His word for the occasion. People respond and there comes faith to deal effectively with enquirers for Salvation. With some of God's servants faith is used under God in distribution of gifts. I have observed that there is very real diversity of ministry and function amongst God's people as the Spirit is in action. Some are used deeply and regularly in certain spheres and only intermittently, or not at all, in other spheres. Others again may be mightily gifted in areas where the first are lacking. Let each man fulfil his own ministry.

In addition to the functions mentioned I would like to relate one of my own earlier experiences in relation to faith—about which, I may say, I knew very little at the time concerned. Some time after my Baptism in the Spirit I was on the hills behind Greenock one day when I had a very powerful urge to preach the gospel. I looked over the town and was drawn to one particular part, but not being Greenock-born, I did not recognise the area. So strong, however, was the urge that I came down from the hillside and sought the place indicated. What was my surprise—or rather consternation—to find there, nothing but a beautiful red sandstone church. I stood across the street and thought, 'You can't go to another man and ask for the use of his building to preach the gospel,' and I went away in bewilderment. But I could not put the impression out of my mind. It remained there for years. I looked around to find other buildings nearby—but nothing else quite fitted. It was that building. One day at the end of a teaching session in school a pupil who had recently been converted in one of our services, approached me and said, 'Mr Black, our church is closing. Would you be interested in it?' I said, 'What church is that, lad?' 'Oh,' he said, 'the red sandstone church in West Stewart Street, in Greenock.' 'Do you go to a Greenock church?' I asked. (This conversation was taking place in a Port Glasgow school.) 'Yes' he said, 'my folks have always belonged to that church.' 'Well,' I said, 'as it happens I am interested in that church. Will you keep me in touch as decisions are made?' He came back soon after to tell me that the deacons had met again and decided to continue for another year, and so the matter dropped.

Almost exactly a year later I was walking along the main street in Greenock when a gentleman ran after me along the pavement and laid his hand on my arm. 'Mr Black,' he said, 'our church is closing. Would you be interested?' Now, although I knew this gentleman, I did not know his church connection. 'What church is that, Robert?' I asked. 'Oh, sure you know—the red sandstone church in West Stewart Street.' I really was shaken this time. I said, 'You are the second person who has asked me that question and as it happens I am interested in that church, and it is the only church I have ever been interested in and I have been interested in it for years. What are you going to do? Will you let it?' 'No,' he replied, 'we have had a final meeting and it is going to be sold.' 'Well, Robert,' I said. 'I want the church but we have no money.' 'That,' he said, 'is a pity for it must be sold and if you want the church you'll need money.' I went away perhaps a little excited but not particularly hopeful. We were at that time a very small company—about a dozen. We had never had any thought of owning a church and had not gathered funds for such a purpose. We had, in fact, about £50 and the proposition seemed impossible. 'Well,' I thought, 'I'll see if we can raise a loan from a building society.' And as it happened, I was on the eve of departure for Lewis where I was expecting to remain for a lengthy period. 'Still,' I thought, 'I can deal with building societies as easily from there as from here' and went north. I then discovered, first, that there was a credit squeeze at the time and, second, that building societies were not prepared to advance money to churches or clubs. So I phoned my bank manager who informed me that if we could raise a third of the total amount it might be possible to get private individuals to loan the remainder. The bank itself was not interested. I then phoned the lawyer who was acting for the sellers and asked him to act for us too. The closing date was imminent but he extended it by a month in order to let me get home again to deal with the matter.

I came home and spoke to our group. One of them gave a gift of £100 and a loan of another £100 which became a gift. This took us to the princely sum of £250 for a building insured for over £16,000, and we were within about forty-eight or seventy-two hours of the deadline. Then the miracles began—or perhaps I should say—continued. A gentleman came to me on a Sunday afternoon and offered to loan us up to £1,000 (at only nominal interest and for a fifteen year period) to buy the church. Prior to that day he would not have given £1 for this purpose—but a crisis had taken place in his life an hour before he saw me—a crisis I may say in which I was in no way involved—and he had the desire to take this step. So £1,250 was now available.

I phoned the lawyer, and being a farmer's son, and since I was acting for the church and was unwilling to give more that I had to, I asked him if he would be interested in an offer of £750. 'No,' he said. 'But make it £850 and I'll do what I can for you.' He phoned back within twenty-four hours to tell us that the building with everything in it was ours.

Now a less suitable church in a less suitable site had been sold to a business firm for £3,000 just shortly before this, but in the case of our building, I understand, the church officials divided applicants into three categories: (a) churches and religious organisations, (b) clubs, (c) businesses. Their cause was coming to an end in Greenock and they were not particularly interested in money. They much preferred the building to go on being used as a church rather than to be used for other purposes. I believe four religious groups showed an interest but for various reasons the other three dropped out and the church was ours. My lawyer, not himself a professed evangelical, told me a strange thing. 'From the beginning,' he said, 'I felt you should get that church.'

The miracles continued. The gentleman who offered the £1,000 went to his accountant to make arrangements for raising the money and as he waited in the ante-room for his appointment he recognised the footstep of one of his own brothers in the flesh going out of the accountant's office. This brother had a very distinctive footstep—one leg being half an inch shorter than the other. As it happened there had been a business loan of thousands of pounds between the two brothers for years and one of them had, without the other's knowledge, chosen to repay part of the loan on that day through their common accountant. Thus, when the gentleman making the loan to the church went in, the thousand pounds was sitting there on the table—or at least the arrangement for securing it was there. He did not have to disturb a single investment or account. Note the timing, there was not even one other client at the accountant between the appointments of the two brothers. Some people might call this coincidence—others would call it God.

Note the events: a vision on the hillside; the seeking of the place of vision and the finding of a church; the approach from a pupil about that church; the approach of a deacon about the same building; the attitude of the lawyer; the offer of the money in the nick of time; the experience of the two brothers with the accountant. Finally, we secured the building in time to take literally thousands of people to the Billy Graham Campaign in Kelvin Hall in 1955 and from the buses run, scores professed conversion. I repeat, some people call this kind of thing coincidence—others call it God!

It is not my purpose here to give the whole history of our

church. (Nor indeed do I claim this to be a full history of this part of our development. It represents events as seen by me and in which I was involved. There were others involved too and their stories might well contain other vital details.) I would, however, like to carry the story two stages further.

Shortly after we were settled God gave another forward urge. I envisaged a further three churches in the area and had plans drawn up for the first of these. Again we had no money but proceeded as though we had. On a New Year's eve I was again approached by a gentleman who offered to sell his stocks and shares and loan us the proceeds to erect a second church. The amount realised was exactly the amount of the estimate for the new church. It was built. An urge grew for the next building. I passed the site every day on my way to school and used to feel, 'That site is ours.' Ultimately we got it, but again we had no money and, moreover, God told me we would not get money for this building or the next in the way that had previously happened. He did tell me, however, to investigate the Covenant Scheme. 'But,' I said, 'I have already done this and my accountant has told me that only people paying tax at standard rate are eligible.' Our congregation at the time was young and the bulk of the people were paying at lower rates. I had thought earlier that such payments should be reclaimable but my accountant had been quite definite—the answer was, 'No!'. But here was God saying, 'Investigate the Covenant Scheme.' So I obeyed God. I bypassed the accountant and went directly to an Inspector of Taxes, who very graciously showed me how all tax that our people were paying was recoverable. He took time to show me exactly how I should go about things. I put the matter to the church and many immediately joined the scheme.

Difficulties remained and I did something which I had never done before, nor have I ever repeated it. I 'put out a fleece'! I told the people that if a certain sum (far above normal offerings), which I did not disclose, came in on a particular month, I would take that as a sign to start. I asked them to give as God led and not be psychologically influenced. Far above the prescribed amount came in and we commenced. When the building opened it was clear of all debt and indeed, I had the feeling that we had more in the bank then than when we commenced. This I cannot explain. In the same way the next building went up and property after property has been acquired since then as the needs have arisen.

In what way is all this relevant? It illustrates the operation of faith. I do not know how faith came, but come it did—as imperceptible as the dew. About one week before we put in the offer for the first church, while as yet there was no evidence of provision, it came over me—the conviction—I might almost say knowledge, that we would get the building. It came from God. There was nothing of me in it. There was nothing I could do to bring it. But it was very sure—very real. Again over the covenant arrangements there came faith as God indicated what to do. It is quite wonderful to walk with God.

Note

[1] Fee writes, 'While it is true that Paul considers the "faith" that leads to salvation to be the work of the Spirit in the believer's life, what he has in mind here [1 Cor 12:9] is the special gift of supernatural faith that can "move mountains," mentioned again in 13:2. It probably refers to a supernatural conviction that God will reveal his power or mercy in a special way in a specific instance.' Fee, First Epistle to the Corinthians, p.593.

5

The Gifts of Healings

... and to another gifts of healings, in the one Spirit (1 Cor 12:9)

Christians who believe in Divine healing by supernatural, as distinct from natural means, fall into two main groups: (a) those who believe that God has made promises in His Word which give men a warrant to claim healing as of right, when they fulfil particular conditions, which seem attached to the promises and (b) those who believe that God can and sometimes does intervene directly in healing, but who do not consider that He has promised to do so in all cases. In other words this group believes that healing may be received miraculously, but that men may not claim it as an inalienable right.

Both groups are fully persuaded that God does intervene in human health and that healings frequently take place—from very simple to very serious cases. The first group generally take the view that healing is in the atonement and refer frequently to Isaiah 53:4–5 in support. The second group tend to see supernatural healing as something God frequently does, but are more vague in linking this with the atonement—certainly in any universal way.

First, what saith the Scripture? The verses most frequently referred to from the Old Testament are:

> ...I am the Lord that healeth thee (Ex 15:26).

> Surely he hath borne our griefs, and carried our sorrows: yet we did esteem him stricken, smitten of God, and afflicted. But he was wounded for our transgressions, he was bruised for our iniquities: the chastisement of our peace was upon him; and with his stripes we are healed (Is 53:4–5).

> For I will restore health unto thee, and I will heal thee of thy wounds (Jer 30:17).

and from the New Testament:

> ...they shall lay hands on the sick, and they shall recover.' Mark 16. 18. 'And he called the twelve together, and gave them power and authority over all devils, and to cure diseases (Lk 9:1).

> Heal the sick, raise the dead, cleanse the lepers, cast out devils: freely ye received, freely give' (Mt 10:8).

> ...and to another gifts of healings,' in the one Spirit' (1 Cor 12:9).

> Is any among you suffering? let him pray. Is any cheerful? let him sing praise. Is any among you sick? let him call for the elders of the church; and let them pray over him, anointing him with oil in the name of the Lord: and the prayer of faith shall save him that is sick, and the Lord shall raise him up (Jas 5:13–15).

> Who his own self bare our sins in his body upon the tree, that we, having died unto sins, might live unto righteousness; by whose stripes ye were healed (1 Pet 2:24).

In addition healings are cited from the Old and New Testaments. For example, from the life of Elisha, the healing of Naaman from leprosy in 2 Kings 5 and the raising of the Shunamite's son from the dead in 2 Kings 4 are often cited. The New Testament abounds with instances. The ministry of Christ is heavily weighted on this side. Healings, including the raising of the dead, occur in the work of both Peter and Paul.

Thus there can be no doubt of the fact of healing in Bible times. The question remains—does it still happen? Any sincere enquirer who cares to peruse the growing body of literature on this subject, with its many well-documented cases of healing, can hardly be left in doubt. In Britain, during the earliest part of the century, amongst those deeply used in the ministry were George and Stephen Jeffreys and Smith Wigglesworth. In America, Dr Charles Price and Kathryn Kuhlman were much used. There have been, and are, of course, many others. Healing too has been a prominent feature of the moving of the Spirit in Korea and Indonesia in very recent times. Evidence is not difficult to come by. Indeed it is there in abundance. In this work, however, I prefer to speak of things of which I have personal knowledge—rather than quote from the writings and experiences of others.

My interest in healing preceded my own Baptism in the Spirit. I found growing in me a great compassion for people in ill-health and a real excitement at the prospect of healing in cases where doctors could do no more. Faith grew as I studied the Bible. I read *The Ministry of the Miraculous* by E. C. W. Boulton and *Ever Increasing Faith* and *Smith Wigglesworth Apostle of Faith*. As I read, I became increasingly convinced of the reality and the possibility of healing; but, at the same time, I saw no healing around me, and this despite loud claims to belief in healing. This perplexed me and indeed some of the things which I ultimately witnessed alarmed me. Many of my friends took the view: healing is in the Bible—all we have to do is claim it, and claim it they frequently did and it just did not work. This was bad and bad enough—but as time passed and I became acquainted with the work of certain evangelists it seemed to me that exaggerated claims were being made, and sometimes to explain failure, blame was put on the lack of faith of sufferers. People would be encouraged to come for ministry. They would be prayed for and told they were healed. Generally this was not the case and they were then left not only with their original illnesses but with confused minds. If, and when, it was suggested that their faith was deficient, or perhaps that there was unconfessed sin in their lives, their plight was very sad indeed. I do not remember the persons praying suggesting that there might have been any weakness in their ministries. All of this I found very unsatisfactory.

One particular case brought matters to a head. 'Revival and Healing' campaigns were frequently held in those days. Many evangelists may have felt it incumbent upon them to pray for the sick; and, in my view, as some of them did so, the sense of God in a gathering could be felt to diminish. This caused me no problem. I simply felt that they did not have healing ministries and were mistaken in their approach. There came, however, one evangelist who did have a healing ministry. As he began to pray for the sick I could sense the deepening of the atmosphere—the awareness of the presence of God. He invited sufferers to come to the front and there he laid hands on them. All were told that they were healed. As he prayed I sometimes felt a quickening of faith in my own spirit for particular individuals, perhaps numbers one and seven in a line of twelve. It might emerge later that one and seven were healed but the others not. I asked him if he did not himself have a witness when a person was being healed. 'Oh yes,' he said, 'I do.' 'Then why,' I asked, 'do you tell all the others that they too are healed?' 'Well,' he said, 'you don't want to discourage them or destroy their faith, do you? And in any case God might heal them.' I replied, 'Destroy their faith—surely what you are doing now is just that! If you prayed for all, but only indicated that those would be healed for whom you had revelation or faith, surely people would come to feel that they were receiving the Word of God through you and real faith would be greatly quickened.' I went on, 'I don't know what things are like elsewhere, but you are in Scotland now and I know how a Scotsman's mind works. If you tell ten people that they are healed and nine actually are and one is not, a Scotsman wants to know why you told a lie in the case of the one.' I do not think my friend appreciated my remarks but I have never felt I had any cause to regret or retract them. There should be scrupulous honesty in the ministry. Again and again pastors have to help people who are left deeply disappointed after such campaigns come to an end. The matter was not glorifying to God.

I observed, too, that particular evangelists with healing ministries were able to stimulate real faith as they preached. Their ministries were real and healings did take place. I fear, however, that sometimes they wrongly assumed teaching mantles when teaching was not their gift or calling. In short, as practitioners they were good: as teachers they could mislead others. At that time the teaching was widespread that healing was for all, that it was in the atonement and could be universally claimed. The healers departed. Their teaching remained, and the very unhappy position arose of sufferers being encouraged to believe, to ignore the evidence of their senses, to go on believing and finally to be shut in with their infirmities and sometimes with deep psychological problems added. Thus at an early stage I found it necessary to distinguish between a man's accomplishments in a field to which he was manifestly called, and his own views relative to that field. In short, a man might be used in healing but have very defective views about the doctrine of healing.

I read the literature; I heard the claims; I saw some people healed; I saw many unhealed. I studied the Bible and experienced personal healing and was used in the healing of others and my views became clearly defined. I was unhappy with the teaching that we could demand healing as of right. In the first place, it did not work and in the second, it was inconsistent with the doctrine of death to self and the principle, 'I live; and yet no longer I, but Christ liveth in me.' The initiative surely must always be with God. In so far as healing is for me, I must be dependent on His action and where I may be used for others again I must look to Him to move through me. This whole approach I found to be God-glorifying. I had early recognised that no man could be saved when he liked. He was totally dependent on the 'blowing of the wind'—on the action of the Holy Spirit. He could, by God's grace, respond—he could not initiate. Thus I found it to be in healing.

So against the tide of the more general view in Pentecostal circles I maintained this position and found that God in His great graciousness did move in healing power. We had no formula. We observed that while many teachers tried to produce hard and fast rules, Christ Himself had no set pattern. He sometimes spoke a word as in the case of the Centurion's servant (Mt 8:5–13). He made clay and anointed a man's eyes (Jn 9:1–12). He demanded faith as in the case of the woman with the issue of blood (Mt 9:20–22). On the other hand he raised the dead as in the case of Lazarus where there was neither faith in the dead man, nor in the mourners. In short healing did not always happen in the same way. In the case of the blind man from Bethsaida (Mk 8:22–26) it came in two stages. In the case of the nobleman's son (Jn 4:46–54) the question was asked, 'When did he begin to amend?' In other cases healing was immediate and dramatic, as, for example, in the case of blind Bartimaeus (Mk 10:46–52), or the case of the lame man lowered through a roof by four friends (Jn 5:8). In some cases all were healed and all manner of diseases departed. In Mark 6:56 we read that 'as many as touched him were made whole.' I observed the danger of taking particular incidents and the instructions of Christ with reference to them and building a universal pattern on them. It was obvious that other cases did not fit the pattern.

The human mind (and indeed the spiritual mind), however, does seek underlying principles and laws that govern total situations, and in my view the underlying principle in this case is very clear and very simple. Christ wrought His miracles by the power of the Holy Spirit. He was led of the Spirit. He moved in the Spirit. The Spirit operated through Him and in the Spirit there is often wonderful variety and diversity of working. He knew the needs of every individual. He did that which was exactly appropriate in every case—whether to stimulate faith, or produce an act of obedience, or bring a person to life when death had already occurred. In my view those of us who are used in healing should so live in the Spirit that we are sensitive to His slightest touch. We should do exactly what He says—or rather we should allow Him unrestricted flow and action through us.

This does remind me of Kathryn Kuhlman, of whom I have written in *Reflections on the Baptism in the Holy Spirit*. She had discovered this secret and was deeply used in healing. On the one occasion on which I heard her, I remember her saying before preaching, 'I am going to speak to you today about the Holy Spirit. Now I may not be able to finish the sermon. If He comes on me in a particular way I must obey Him.' That obedience had to be instantaneous and complete. The Spirit was in action. She was only a channel. She did finish the sermon; He did come upon her and wonderful and numerous healings did take place. So far as I have been able to trace, Miss Kuhlman did not write much about the theory of healing but in a few telling pages she expressed similar views to those outlined here. She, too, had been desperately disappointed at much that was happening in 'Healing' meetings and looked to God for better things. She was not disappointed.

Before knowing Kathryn Kuhlman, my own experiences had witnessed to God moving in these ways. Shortly after my Baptism in the Spirit I was engaged in heavy manual work and strained a hip on a day before an important conference. I had much preparation to do in the evening and found that I was in such pain that I could not concentrate properly. As I read of healing in *The Ministry of the Miraculous* by Boulton, suddenly there came with great clarity a thought—as of a bolt from the blue—'God could heal you now.' With the thought came the deed. All pain died out of my body. I changed chairs again and again to see if I could find it again—but no, it was truly gone. To say I was shocked is putting it mildly. The great God had come so very close.

One of the early cases in which another was healed contains an important principle. I had been engaged in school teaching for a short time and some of my pupils had found Christ. The young sister of one of them was ill and I went to visit her. There, for the first time, I met the grandmother who was herself a Christian. Just before leaving I learned that she had suffered from arthritis for many years and was in real distress. I asked her if she would like me to pray for her and was assured that she would. We got down on our knees and suddenly God dealt—not with her—but with me. He brought sharply to my consciousness an area of my life where there was a distinct shadow between Him and me. I called it shadow: He called it sin and I acknowledged it. I was willing to be sorted out and He generously took it away. Immediately I rose and laid hands on the old lady and prayed for her. It seems she was instantaneously healed. To the day of her death, many years later, she never suffered from arthritis again. Had I prayed before being fully through to God myself I do not believe she would have been one whit the better of it. To my mind it is of prime importance that God's channels be in the right place with Him with no unconfessed and unforgiven sin lurking in the background—even if it does masquerade under the name of 'shadow'. From this incident I learned an important lesson I have never forgotten.

The next incident also has unusual features and again relates to a boy, Hugh, who had been one of my pupils— oddly enough the special friend of Roy, the lad who featured in the last incident. Hugh had one brother and one sister and he came from a very irreligious home. By this time he had left school and married as had his sister. His young brother had also found Christ, but endured a good deal of unpleasantness from his brother-in-law who was a professed atheist or agnostic. One day Hugh came to me to say that his brother-in-law had been injured at work. A metal filing had gone into an eye and he had been rushed to hospital. Things were very bad. The surgeon feared that the eye might have to be taken out because of the danger of the other eye being affected. I asked Hugh if he would like me to go in and pray for him—although I had never met him and was also well aware of his views. On being assured that he would, we gathered around his bed one Tuesday night—Hugh and his wife, the young man's wife and myself. I asked if he would mind if I read a short portion from the Bible—to this he agreed. I then laid hands on him and prayed very briefly and immediately came away.

Shortly afterwards I learned that he professed to having felt something happen in his eye on the moment of prayer. When the nurse next changed the bandage she noticed a change and reported it. Within a very short time he was out of hospital with no operation, but with two perfectly good eyes which he has to this day. In the words of the young atheist—his words—not mine, 'Mr Black's God healed me.' He was not, and is not, a Christian. I have never seen him again. He has never visited the church. How do you explain it? Just note that Christ healed people who were not His followers. Ours, to obey the Holy Spirit and not introduce our own rules. God healed that young man—that is God's business. I have prayed for many fine Christians who have not been healed. That too is God's business. I may lay hands on two people at the same time and know God is healing one and not the other. I do not know why—but that too is God's business. Learn to obey the Spirit and neither add to nor take away anything from His action.

While some people who seek healing have great difficulty in opening themselves to it, others seem to be peculiarly 'healable' (if I may invent a word). The next two cases fall into this category. One young lady who had recently been baptised in the Spirit suffered very severely from hay fever. Summers were agony to her and she had little or no relief through medication. On being prayed for very simply she was immediately healed and so far as I know never suffered from the affliction again. This same lady was leaving the church one Saturday night and on the way out mentioned that she would not be present in the morning. She had fallen on the frozen street on her way to church and was in considerable pain. With no thought of healing, I asked her to hold on for a minute or two and I would give her a run home. I was thinking solely of her injured back. Had I thought of praying for her I would have done it in the church. When, however, we were half-way to her house it suddenly occurred to me to pray and that put me in a predicament. It is one thing laying hands on a young lady in the presence of others in a church—it is another to do this privately in a car parked by the roadside at night. Passers-by might just possibly misunderstand. What was I to do?

The feeling to pray was strong and I took what you might think to be a coward's way out. I thought, 'I will not lay hands on her but I could take an elbow with my left hand— and nobody will be able to see that.' Suddenly all these problems were totally forgotten. Never shall I forget that hour. I have seen many healings and some from far more desperate conditions than this one, but never, I think, one more dramatic. Christ Himself seemed to come into that car and the blood drained from the face of the lady as what I might almost call the shock hit her. 'Where has the pain gone?' she said. 'It has all drained out of my body.' It was immediate and wonderful. The presence of Christ was glorious.

The second case of this type related to an older lady—a very mature Christian who had been in His service for many years. The first of Dorothy's healings was of a stomach condition of long-standing. She had arrived at a conference in considerable pain and this was getting worse. At that time she did not know us very well and she was reluctant to ask for prayer for healing. Ultimately, however, she was persuaded. The prayer was simple and brief and she retired to bed. Suddenly she realised that all pain had gone and she was perfectly well. In her excitement she went into a friend's room to share the news. Her friend, Ann, leapt out of bed to hug her, and as she did so, an ear condition from which she had long suffered and which was not responding to treatment was immediately healed. Dorothy tends to be accident prone and again and again God has stepped in to heal. Of all the people I have ever met she is perhaps the one who, from one point of view, seems to be most easily healed.

The remark, 'Where has the pain gone?' reminds me of another case in which the same element of shocked surprise occurred. On one occasion I was ministering in an Assembly of God in Nottingham and had an invitation to visit the home of a godly couple who attended another church. On a previous visit I had discovered that the husband had been baptised in the Spirit but that the wife—a sister of two ladies who had been deeply used of God in revival in Congo—had certain reservations. On this visit I found her desperate to receive the experience. In a very short time that afternoon she was baptised gloriously. In the evening she, her husband and her daughter of about eighteen came along to the service at which I was preaching. I felt a very strong urge to preach on healing that night—which was out of line with the subjects I had previously taken. I had no knowledge of anybody present being in any particular need but the urge was unmistakable. I preached and immediately afterwards asked those seeking healing to indicate the fact, but to remain in their seats. To my surprise the daughter raised her hand. I came down from the platform and quietly prayed for her. I had only moved about a yard away when the commotion broke out behind me. She was in a state of considerable agitation—as one searching for something that has been lost—which indeed she was. 'What has happened?' I asked. She said, 'I don't know. I have had a lump under my arm and when you prayed it suddenly disappeared and I can't find it. Where did it go?' A very human and understandable question. She went on to add, 'For about a year I have had something wrong with one foot as well and it has been healed too.' When a healing is like this—instantaneous and involving the sudden disappearance of observable physical matter, or the sudden creation of new matter, I think it is almost impossible for the person to whom it happens to remain quiet. The reality breaks through them and others are tremendously affected.

Sometimes healings take place in a service without anyone praying for the individual concerned. One such case was Helen, a senior nurse. During the course of her work her back had been damaged. Discs had slipped and she had undergone an operation unsuccessfully. The condition caused her great pain. I remember her having to lie flat on the floor of a little room off the main conference hall at our Summer camp—listening to services. She faced a serious situation professionally and was faced with a further possible operation whose chance of success was only rated at 50/50. The operation was regarded as very serious. There came a night towards the close of one meeting when she was with us in the hall and evidently God spoke to her. He simply said, 'I am going to heal you now.' I happened to be watching her as the service drew to an end with glorious singing. Obviously something extraordinary was happening. It was glorious. She was totally healed in a few moments—from the crown of her head to the soles of her feet. It was complete. She shortly afterwards demonstrated her ability to touch her toes and never again has her back troubled her.

As I look back over the years there have been so many glorious moments that should be recorded. I may indeed prepare a book with others speaking for themselves: Una healed wonderfully on several occasions—bathed in the power of God—and her sister, Fiona, healed on one occasion by the laying on of hands and very dramatically on another when anointed with oil and having the reality of 'the prayer of faith' offered on her behalf. In this case the doctor was delighted. The healing saved a hysterectomy and has been permanent. Her story is too good for me to give in truncated form. Much better to have it in a separate publication—although I have not asked her about that yet!

One final case: a number of years ago the winter in Scotland was particularly severe and a man found himself driving his tractor on a fairly narrow path above a steep valley. He did not realise that his brakes were frozen until he tried to apply them. They had no effect at all. The tractor toppled over the edge and he went down with it, being pinned underneath as it rolled on top of him. Three ribs were broken, his stomach was crushed, his spleen ruptured and he suffered great loss of blood. He was alone when the accident occurred and hours passed before he was discovered. Sub-zero temperatures persisted throughout the time he lay injured. Ultimately he was found and rushed to hospital. The news came to me as I was teaching and there came on me an almost unbearable burden. With the close of school I went quickly home and prepared to leave for hospital. As I was about to drive off I noticed that I had forgotten my Bible—which I normally take with me on hospital visitation. So strong was the urge to have it that I went back upstairs to collect it. I finally arrived at hospital and reached the sixth floor—at the very top—when I realised that I had left the Bible in the car. Rather than face the stairs again I decided to go in. There he lay, pale as death against the white sheets and again the urge came on me to get my Bible. So strong was it that I excused myself to the Sister and went back downstairs. When I returned I just opened the Bible and read from where my eyes fell:

> Thus saith the Lord God unto these bones: Behold, I will cause breath to enter into you, and ye shall live. And I will lay sinews upon you, and will bring up flesh upon you, and cover you with skin, and put breath in you, and ye shall live; and ye shall know that I am the Lord (Ezek 37:5–6).

I could not but note the appropriateness of the words. There he lay with broken ribs and ruptured spleen. His pulse when found had almost gone. Blood transfusions by this time had been given. He had been X-rayed but no operation had taken place. He was expected to die. As I read, something happened inside me. There came a moment of faith, a realisation that God Himself was speaking—I read the portion again and again and faith became absolute. 'You are going to live,' I said. 'You are not going to die. God has just spoken to me.' The man later told me that when he was prayed for, it was as though a hand passed across his abdomen. I left the bed and sought the doctor who was on duty. I asked her for a medical assessment. It was indeed grave. She gave me to understand that he was suffering from a number of injuries any one of which could prove fatal and one of which always was fatal—the ruptured spleen. So again I found myself in a situation where man said one thing and God another. I then went to the home of the doctor who had admitted the man to hospital and who happened to be a member of our own congregation—very recently saved and baptised in the Spirit. I said, 'I want you to tell me about this patient but before you say anything let me say quite definitely that no matter what you say I know that he is going to live.' I told her of what had happened. 'Now,' I said, 'I am asking for the sake of his family who, although Christians, are not likely to take encouragement from what I have just told you.' Her face was a study. It was evident that from a medical point of view things were very serious indeed.

By a strange coincidence the Sister who had admitted the man to her ward was the girl referred to earlier, whose grandmother had been healed of arthritis and who was also a member of our church. She knew of my involvement in the case and hoped to be off duty by the time I arrived at hospital. She did not want to be the one to tell me of his death! I waited for two days and went back to see him. Again by a strange coincidence I did not have my Bible, but by this time his own was by his bedside and I used it. Again I opened at random and from quite a different place found my eye fall on the words 'he shall surely live, he shall not die' (Ezek 18:21). Some might call this coincidence, others call it God.

In short, he was out of hospital in a remarkably brief time. He was never operated on. His ribs came together and he was back at manual work in which he remained until he was sixty-five. He was as strong as before his accident and

83

lived to seventy-five. The doctor mentioned has again and again given public testimony to this miracle of healing. The case went right against the books. Man said, 'He will die.' God said, 'He will not die but live.' As always God was right—glory be to His Name.

There is an interesting end to this story. Years later I was giving a series of addresses on the miraculous to my senior pupils. On the last of these I told this story without mentioning my own part in it. One lad, then my vice-captain and later a member of staff, came to me and said, 'I think I know about that case. I am friendly with a nurse who works in Greenock Royal Infirmary. She is an atheist but something that happened one day has disturbed her views. There was a man who had a tractor accident who should have died—but he didn't die.' 'Yes,' I said, 'it is the same case. It is perfectly true.'

Now observe, there was no power in me to heal. I could not initiate the healing. Indeed I could do nothing at all, and to have tried to act myself would just have been ludicrous. I was wholly dependent on God. I had to do what He asked—bear a burden, get a Bible, listen to what He said from it and believe His word, witness to the patient and the doctor and rejoice in the outcome. It was all of God, and I felt then as I feel now, that I had nothing to do with it. 'Why,' you say, 'did God heal in this case?' I almost wrote, 'I don't know.' But in fact at the time I did get a flash and I think there was something very particular that God wanted done through that man—but in many cases I do not know. Why are some not healed? I do not always know, but I do believe in the sovereignty of God and leave it there.

Where does all this leave us in relation to healing generally and the gifts of healings in particular? Perhaps in closing this chapter, a number of points can be emphasised.

1. It should be noted that a double plural is used in connection with this gift. It is not the 'gift of healing' but

'gifts of healings'. This suggests what I think is borne out in experience, that different people may be particularly used in particular areas of illness. Some, for example, may find that arthritic sufferers are frequently healed and certain other categories remain comparatively unaffected.[2] As with the gifts of tongues, which is also a double plural, an individual with tongues may suddenly receive quite a new tongue. So, I believe, new gifts of healings may come on that same person from time to time. I have found that in areas of a man's ministry in which God moves regularly and powerfully, faith grows and the work prospers. There are other areas in which there seems to be little, or no movement. Give glory to God for this too. It is the Spirit who distributes gifts and it is as He wills. His object is to glorify Christ. Ours may too often be to glorify ourselves.

2. The evidence of the Bible shows unequivocally that God did heal in the past and that His children were encouraged to bring their needs before Him in this, as in other, fields. There is abundant evidence in present day literature and experience to persuade sincere seekers after truth of the reality of healing and to encourage them to seek it positively. There should indeed be a very positive attitude to healing. It seems reasonable to me to assume that God generally desires to heal his children unless there is a specific reason for healing being withheld.

3. Gifts are to be used, and can only properly be used, under the anointing of the Holy Spirit. God has not given the initiative in this or in other spiritual matters into human hands. We are not in a position to demand of God.[1] We ought rather to seek the mind of God and allow the Holy Spirit to move through us whether in relation to our own healing, or to the healing of others. This is consistent with the doctrine of death to self. Failure to observe this principle has led to much confusion over healing and brought discredit on an aspect of Christian work which was intended to be

wholly God-glorifying. Satan has won victories here.

4. We should recognise that God may sometimes say No for His own sovereign purposes. We do not read that Epaphroditus who was 'sick nigh unto death' (Phil 2:27) had a special healing. Paul told Timothy, 'Use a little wine for thy stomach's sake and thine often infirmities' (1 Tim 5:23) and he himself, after thrice approaching God on a particular problem, was left with a 'thorn in the flesh' and told that God's grace was sufficient for him. Whether the 'thorn' referred to a particular physical ailment or not we are not told but the principle lying behind the incident is very clear. The initiative was not with Paul but with God. In modern times some of God's choicest saints have also suffered ill-health, even those who have believed that God could, and often did, heal.[3]

5. The teaching that healing is for all, at all times, and should be universally claimed, obviously does not work, and as a result, when over-insisted on, brings reproach on the Work. Much harm has been done in this way and many people have been hurt as a result. To make this claim goes beyond what can be proved from Scripture and may indeed turn people away from seeking healing altogether.

6. Exaggerated claims should be avoided. It is often wise to have a healing confirmed by the passage of time and the report of a doctor before giving it too great publicity. It should also be realised that the very psychological effect of being prayed for may cause a temporary change in symptoms. This should not be regarded as healing. Sufferers are sometimes so anxious to be healed, that they are ready to believe that this has happened before anything significant has really occurred.

7. While it is wise to have healings confirmed before they are given undue publicity, it is also recognised that God sometimes demands faith from an individual before there is any outward evidence of change in his condition. Indeed at

times He may go further and require a person to testify to what is going to happen before it has, in fact, taken place. This can apply to healing and, when God is in the matter, it always works. The danger rises when human imagination replaces Divine guidance, and claims are based on human hope rather than on the revelation of God.

8. A wise and balanced approach should be adopted. All the encouragement that the Word gives should be given. The person with the ministry should be open to God to bring the benefits to the sufferer. A clear explanation of the instrument's dependence on God, and explanation of how God operates, can be very helpful to a person seeking healing and this can help to prevent leaving broken hearts behind.

9. Careful study should be given to James 5:14–15. Note that elders are involved here and a church setting is envisaged. Man still cannot initiate action. The faith must come from God—but when it comes it is effective. The possibility of sin causing the sufferer's condition is indicated and confession can be a necessary condition of healing. Avoid the danger of reading into this Scripture that faith can come by human will or desire. We open ourselves to it but the coming of real faith and healing power is from God alone and this we cannot alter, no matter how hard, or frequently, we try. On the other hand, the encouragement given here is very positive and in a church, moving with God, and increasingly as spiritual life deepens, we should expect to see healings becoming the rule rather than the exception as a result of praying for the sick.

10. It should be noted that healings may be gradual or instantaneous. In the former case a gift of healing may be in operation along with the gift of faith. In the latter the gift of miracle also seems to be involved. Frequently several gifts are involved in one operation. Because a healing may be gradual from the point when prayer is made makes it no less

supernatural. When the healing is instantaneous the miraculous element, of course, is much more apparent.

There is enough in the Bible and in experience to encourage the sufferers and the servants of God who are used in this ministry. There is also enough to discourage the impetuous and foolhardy who would try to manipulate God and take the reins into their own hands. Experience has proved the folly of so doing. We are left with man being nothing—the small dust in the balance and God being all in all.

Notes

[1] Fee comments that 'the early church lived in regular expectation that God would heal people's physical bodies. This expectation was based in part on the OT promises that in the messianic age God would "heal" his people. Only among the intellectuals and in a "scientific age" is it thought to be too hard for God to heal the sick.' In a footnote he adds: '...this is also unfortunately true of many contemporary Christians, whose theology has made a severe disjunction between the "then" and "now" of God's working. This seems to be a seriously flawed understanding of the kingdom, which according to the NT was inaugurated by Christ in the power of the Spirit, who continues the work of the kingdom until the consummation.' Fee, *First Epistle to the Corinthians*, p.594.

[2] Fee makes another suggestion—'that each occurrence is a "gift" in its own right' (*ibid.*). I am not happy with this.

[3] I remember being amazed at the attitude of a lady who, although very deeply used of God, had suffered much ill-health for many years. She came to a crisis of pain in her illness and when things were at their height Christ came to her and asked if she wanted to be healed. Her answer was amazing, 'If it is Your will.' Immediately she was healed totally from the crown of her head to the soles of her feet. Notice the spiritual attitude— the will of God was paramount. This is how life should be lived.

6

The Gift of Miracles

Miracles in general and the Gift of Miracles in particular

...and to another workings of miracles (1 Cor 12:10)

Miracle in this context may be defined as the suspension or alteration of the normal laws of nature by Divine intervention and may range from relatively minor to major matters. When miracles are mentioned most people immediately think of events such as the Red Sea crossing, or the plagues upon Egypt, or Shadrach, Meshach and Abed-nego coming unscathed from the burning fiery furnace. These indeed were miracles but there were many other less dramatic things in the Bible which were also miraculous—such as the sign Eliezer sought and received for the recognition of Isaac's bride, Rebecca.

Secondly, miracles are frequently noted in Scripture without any suggestion that the gift of miracles was in operation through any individual—for example in the coming of the chariot of fire to take Elijah up to Heaven or the speaking of the ass to Balaam.

Perhaps in a study of the subject it is wise to list a number of the miracles, and the types of miracles, from Bible times with which most Christians are familiar, for example the creation of the world, the creation of Adam and then of Eve, the flood in Noah's day, the sun standing still in Joshua's day, Daniel's deliverance from the lions. The life of Christ abounds with them: the turning of the water into wine, the healing of the sick, the raising of the dead, the stilling of the storm, walking on water, the multiplication of the loaves and fishes, the exorcism of demons. From the Resurrection (which was itself a miracle) onwards into the era of the Early Church miracles continued. Peter was miraculously directed to Cornelius, who, in turn, was miraculously prepared for his coming. Paul's conversion contained a miraculous element (which, of course, all true conversions do, to some extent). Again Ananias was similarly prepared for his coming. The man who was caught up to the third heaven had a miraculous experience. This was probably Paul himself on the occasion when he was stoned and left for dead. His rising up and walking was again miraculous.

A study of church history shows clearly that miracles continued beyond Bible times. For example Irenaeus could write:

> Even among the brethren frequently in a case of necessity, when a whole Church united in much fasting and prayer, the Spirit has returned to the ex-animated body, and the man was granted to the prayers of the saints.
>
> ...Some, indeed, most certainly and truly cast out demons. So that frequently those persons themselves that were cleaned from wicked spirits, believed and were received into the Church. Others have the knowledge of things to come, as also visions and prophetic communications: others heal the sick by the imposition of hands, and restore them to health. And moreover, as we said above, even the dead have been raised, and continued with us many years. And why should we say more? It is impossible to tell the number of gifts the Church throughout the world received from God, and the deeds performed in the name of Jesus Christ.

...As we hear many of the brethren in the Church who have prophetic gifts, and who speak in all tongues through the Spirit, and who also bring to light the secret things of men for their benefit, and who expound the mysteries of God.[1]

In modern times there is an ever-expanding body of literature with well-documented cases of miracle. In addition to the many cases of healing, exorcism and baptism in the Spirit (all of which, strictly speaking, are miraculous)[2] we learn from time to time of incidents which more accurately fit most people's conception of the phenomenal: for example, the well-authenticated appearance of the vision of a lamb behind Stephen Jeffreys when he preached in Llanelly. The picture remained on the wall for six hours and was seen by hundreds of people. In the ministry of Watchman Nee there was a case of weather being miraculously affected. Abundant rain came in answer to prayer.[3] In an earlier day Finney prayed for rain in a time of long and exceptional drought. Before his service ended the sound of the rain on the roof almost drowned out his voice.

More recently reports have been coming out of Indonesia of extraordinary miracles. Peter and Paul both raised the dead, as did Smith Wigglesworth, but these occasions seem to have been much more rare than what has been happening in Indonesia. In so far as I can discover, although I do not speak with first-hand experience, over thirty-seven cases have been recorded there of the dead being raised. In addition, water has miraculously turned to wine for communion purposes hundreds of times. Miracles have been the order of the day.[4]

I have sought in this book to be topical and concentrate on things about which I have first hand experience rather than merely quote and refer to the experiences of people personally unknown to me, and as I pondered, I realised that I had not seen the dead raised, or water turned to wine, or rivers miraculously having their waters divided; and then I realised that in spite of that, life has been deeply attended by the miraculous. Surely the healings recorded in chapter five are miraculous—the instantaneous ones in the normal sense of the word, the others in the more general sense. The acquisition of the church and churches mentioned in chapter four also contains elements of the miraculous. Chapter three speaks of truly phenomenal events which I witnessed in Lewis. I have known angelic presence and angelic ministry. I have heard a voice from Heaven and have seen demons[5]. Yet as I pondered, I also realised that every time God gives me a clear-cut word to preach (and that is very frequently) a miracle happens. If, on any occasion, it did not happen I would perhaps more deeply appreciate the miraculous nature of what does take place. Every time He uses me in the Baptism in the Spirit for others I am dependent on miracle, as I am for healing and exorcism. Indeed I am persuaded that a Christian, baptised in the Spirit and walking with God, walks daily with miracle. It literally becomes a way of life. Where God is, there is miracle. To my mind, every time the Divine breaks through the natural, sparks fly and miracle takes place. The very walk of a man of God, with God, is miraculous. Frequently overlooked and perhaps amongst the greatest miracles we ever witness is the miracle of conversion. In my view when a soul is rescued from the selfishness and depravity of sin, and truly becomes a lover of God and holiness, a miracle beyond our fathoming takes place. I am reminded of Paul who could write:

> For I am not ashamed of the gospel: for it is the power of God unto salvation to every one that believeth: to the Jew first, and also to the Greek (Rom 1:16).

The figure of speech 'litotes' is used in the phrase 'I am

not ashamed.' It really means, 'I am very proud.' 'What, Paul! Proud of the gospel? In a world which knows the wisdom of Greece and the power and military might of Rome? Don't you realise that Rome crucified your Christ on a Cross? He died as felons die, deserted by a few rag-tag followers.' 'Yes,' I can imagine Paul saying, 'I know. Oh yes, I know—but I know something else. Bring in Lazarus. The philosophers of Greece with all their wisdom could philosophise over his death—speak and write endlessly about it. Christ raised him from the dead with a word. The Caesars ascended the steps to their golden thrones and their steps were the broken bodies of men. He gave His own body to be broken. They sailed through seas of blood to their desired havens. He shed His own blood—but I tell you that what Greece could not do with all its wisdom; what Rome could not do with all its power—Christ can do. He can raise the dead. Where Rome breaks the bodies of men, He recreates them. Rome can trample men in the dust of the gutter. He goes down into the gutters and takes the ship-wrecks of humanity and remakes them. He makes princes of them. Oh, I am proud of the gospel. You see it is the power of God to Salvation. Surely miraculous is the operation.'

Writing this part has brought back memories. The ideas of Christians about the miraculous undoubtedly have subconscious overtones of phenomenal events. Non-Christians, in whose scheme of things the supernatural often does not figure at all, are much more astonished if they meet what we would tend to consider minor miracles, for example in the realm of healing. If I may permit myself a digression I would like to tell of one occasion when I was still quite a young teacher and the question of miracles came up in the staff on which I was serving. There was present a principal teacher of one of the science subjects who was an atheist, or at least an agnostic. He had previously taught me as a pupil and we got on very well. He did not agree with my religious views nor did I with his—but still relations were good. I did not tend to adopt too sanctimonious an attitude with the staff. For example when they were anxious to run a football syndicate and invited me into the pool to bring them luck, as they put it, I did not give them a long lecture on the evils of gambling. Rather I probed the principal teacher of Maths to give an estimate of the chances of winning and then poked fun at 'supposedly educated' people showing such enthusiasm in such a hopeless cause. Moreover I said I would help them—I would keep a record of their doings. This they regarded with suspicion but waited. On the first two weeks the entries ran:

Date   18/– lost beyond recall.
Date   Another 18/– down the drain.

To my consternation they won something on the third week but I was relieved to find it was only 6/– so the entry ran:

Date   Only 12/– lost this week!

And so it went on and good feeling (maybe more on my side than theirs by that time) remained.

Then I remember my form class, whom I took for Religious Education, told me very vociferously that my friend in the science department had been teaching them the theory of evolution and asked how that squared with what I had been telling them. So in the staffroom I said, 'You know, James (name altered here), it's not really quite fair. There you are teaching fourth year evolution upstairs and they take one look at you and decide that right enough it does look as though man and monkeys had a common origin. Isn't it a good job they can come down to me and see a good looking fellow and realise what rubbish it really is!'

This was the kind of background against which the following incident occurred.

The Headmaster had a Bible reading in assembly every morning and on this occasion it was on the loaves and fishes. At lunch-time six of us including the Headmaster and James were at the same table. Now occasionally, if one of us missed assembly another was apt to ask deliberately how the missing member had enjoyed the reading that morning, so, if the Headmaster had not noticed the absence in the morning he was likely to be alerted to it now. This was all in good fun and on this occasion James looked across pointedly at me to say, 'I don't suppose any intelligent person believes that kind of thing nowadays,' referring to the morning reading. At first I said never a word and let them discuss it amongst themselves. However, I was the fish they really wanted to hook, so I waited for my moment and came in. 'Well, James,' I said, 'before speaking of the loaves and fishes I would like to tell you a story I recently heard. A number of scientists were working together and one of them was like yourself, an atheist, and he was causing trouble to one of his colleagues who was a Christian. You realise that not all scientists are unenlightened! There came a day when the Christian set up a very fine solarium. The model worked perfectly showing the sun, moon and planets in motion in their relative positions. His atheist friend was particularly interested in this kind of thing and on discovering it when he came in, was in raptures about it. 'Where did this come from?' he asked the Christian. 'Who made it?' 'It didn't come from anywhere. Nobody made it,' came the reply. The atheist gave his friend a strange look and ultimately became irritated. 'Don't be a fool,' he said. 'It came from somewhere: somebody is bound to have made it.' 'Not at all,' came the reply, until things reached explosion point. Then the Christian took the atheist by the arm to the door and pointing up said, 'Look up there: do you realise that for ages you have been shouting in my ear that the world came from nowhere, it resulted from fortuitous circumstance and nobody made it. You couldn't believe it of that toy on the table indoors—how can you believe it of this glorious creation? A design forever argues a designer.'

As Huxley himself said, 'if the theory of evolution is true it means that there was found floating on the primeval sea of ooze a single cell of protoplasm coming from we know not where, we know not how.'[6] I personally find I cannot believe that and when I put the matter to others and ask the question—had you stood there in the infinitely remote past do you think you would really have believed that one day there would evolve from that single cell an individual who would make you a suitable mate? Surely not! I personally do not have enough faith to believe this kind of thing.

'Now,' I said, 'having cleared the preliminaries, let's deal with the story of the loaves and fishes. In the first place neither of us was there, although you were a good deal nearer the event than me, and I am as unlikely to convince you of the truth of the story as you are to convince me on the other side. Why not be scientific and deal with evidence? Let's leave the loaves and fishes and come up to present day miracles.' I then proceeded to give detail of two of the healings mentioned in chapter five relating to Roy's grandmother and Hugh's brother-in-law. These boys had both been in this school. 'There,' I said, 'there are the names and addresses. This did not happen in India but here in this town. Go and examine the evidence.' I went on from case to case. By this time we were back in the staffroom and a great quietness had descended. Some faces were growing pale. God was there. The bell rang and we went to our classes— but I remember one teacher coming and saying later, 'It's all very well joking about these things in the crowd, but you know, I have a sister dying with cancer. Could your God do anything about that?' Deep in every human heart there lies need and in dealing with our fellows we should always remember it.

Perhaps never until that day did I realise the effectiveness of the evidence of miracle on the unbeliever. With religious theories of many kinds they would argue all day. Real miracle can have a profound effect.

In chapter two, I have already spoken of the miracle which took place in the life of the late Rev Duncan Campbell when he escaped death on his motorbike. I have selected further modern-day cases of which I have close personal knowledge and which fall into the generally accepted category of miracles.

Mr George Reid, who has pastored a Pentecostal work in Glenboig in Scotland for many years, was a paratrooper in the Medical Corps during the war. He came to the moment of his first jump. His group had all received instruction and were ready to go. Some were quite nervous—amongst them, I think, one or two ex-theological students whose views differed from my Pentecostal friend's. He joked with them that they should not be afraid to jump if their theological views were sound and all was well with their souls. 'However,' he said, 'I was last out and it was not so funny when it came to my own turn. I jumped and immediately I knew there was something wrong. There was a great tug on my parachute which should not have happened. I then dropped like a stone and when I pulled my rip cord nothing happened.' Evidently the parachute had become entangled with one of the wheels of the plane and had been ripped right across. 'It was as useless,' he said, 'as a piece of brown paper.' When he realised the perilous nature of his situation he shouted out, 'Lord, here am I.' This I have always found amusing although the circumstances were so serious. It was perfectly obvious where George was. The question was surely rather, where was the Lord? Well, the Lord was there all right. 'I stopped,' said George, 'in mid-air. I didn't just slow down. I stopped and then floated down, having the softest landing I ever had in any parachute jump.' Evidently George landed behind a little hill and he then proceeded to the next point at which he was due to report—the Naafi canteen. As he was having a cup of tea he heard one soldier ask another, 'Who was it who was killed in the parachute jump this afternoon?' The episode had been seen but the hillock had concealed the final stages from some of the watching eyes. The 'blood wagon' had, in fact, been sent to collect the dead man but when it arrived there was no dead man there. Fortunately the whole incident was recorded on film and George received a signed statement confirming the miracle before he left the Services.

The second incident is exceptionally unusual and happened to one of our pastors, Roy, whose grandmother's healing was described in chapter 5. On this occasion he was due to take a meeting at a certain time and found himself delayed at work. He was in a particular office and his watch showed that he was really late. The time to reach his car from where he was would normally be fifteen minutes, and at that point the miracle happened. He does not know how and is unable to explain it. His watch before and after kept perfect time and it had not stopped. Suddenly he was at the second point with no time having elapsed. Had this kind of thing never happened elsewhere I would have hesitated about including it in this book but, while unusual, it is not the first time that such a thing has occurred. In this case the name and address of the person can be supplied and the story investigated. It may remind the reader of Philip who after speaking to the Ethiopian eunuch was found at Azotus (Acts 8:39–40). I seem to remember that David du Plessis has written of a similar experience.

From time to time an unusual and delightful type of miracle occurs when suddenly a room or particular area is flooded with heavenly perfume. First hand reports of this came from some of my friends in Skye a few years ago. On one occasion I myself experienced this miracle in a home in Barvas in Lewis. God had moved powerfully in one family in the Lewis revival. A school teacher and his wife and two sons had been converted. (One son had been the M.C. at the famous dance interrupted by Rev McLennan and Rev Campbell during the Lewis Revival.) The second son then found Christ and all four later experienced the Baptism in the Spirit—the husband and wife receiving in a most unusual way. We had been sitting at the breakfast table when suddenly the power of God fell on us. Now I have seen people go into their Baptism from a state of contrition, some speaking, some singing—but in this case they came with holy laughter (something Wesley experienced). It was a wonderful hour. God continued to bless them and one night at the close of a local house-meeting Mrs MacArthur found herself on a couch beside a nurse who had a back complaint which, if my memory serves me, was not responding to treatment. I was sitting across from them on one side of the peat fire. Suddenly I became aware of spiritual sound— which is another phenomenon often heard when God is moving deeply—it was very distinct. Without knowing of her friend's physical condition Mrs MacArthur placed her hand on her back and began to pray in tongues. Immediately the lady was healed. Of this I had no knowledge at the time—but suddenly I became aware of a most beautiful fragrance as of hyacinth. It filled the room. It is an hour I can never forget.

Much has been written of the Lewis Revival with which the name of the late Rev Duncan Campbell is associated but there was one incident which has not appeared in print and which I heard from his own lips privately. This I found of particular interest. A number of Christians living in a part of the island where things were proving difficult were gathered in prayer. Mr Campbell was present and 'there came,' he said, 'a moment when the break came [i.e. when the victory was won in spiritual places]. I opened my eyes and saw [with natural vision] the demons fly in all directions. [This is very salutary. There the demons had been—obstructing the work of God's people, opposing the coming of revival.] We went out of the hall and the people were coming from all over the community carrying benches. The power of God came and men collapsed on the ground with its coming. Great big men—deeply in sin—were converted.' I include this, not so much for the miracle of Revival with which I wish to deal in another context, but for the fact and the witnessing of the fleeing demons.

The next case is personal and very recent. I was taking the funeral of my son-in-law's father, a very godly Irishman, Mr Robert Gault of Ballymena. I had been with him for some days preceding his death and was present during his actual passing. He was a man who walked with God and knew Him very deeply. Again and again the presence of God was manifest around his bed and his passing was glorious. The whole family shared in the triumph of it. As the time of the funeral approached I felt closed in with God. He was with me in an unusual way. Frequently I find Him powerfully present at funeral services but on this occasion the sense of His Presence was very particular. As I started to take the indoor service I had trouble with my throat. It seemed to be catarrhal and it took a little time before I got reasonable clearance. I may, in fact, in trying to get clarity, have strained my voice a little. When we reached the cemetery, there was a large company of mourners. The wind was blowing and as I began to read I realised I was in real trouble. As I attempted to speak louder in the outdoor conditions I found the position almost impossible. My voice came out as a puny croak. I was desperately frustrated. God had given a word. The power was available and the people were there but the instrument was in a dilapidated state.

Shortly before, I had been writing about Wilkerson in another book and had particularly noted that when he got to the end of his tether in that famous meeting of gangs in *The Cross and the Switchblade*, God came into the situation in a miraculous way. It was as though a voice said to me, 'Well, you know the theory. What about the practice—now? Are you willing to trust God fully?' I must have thrown myself on Him maybe more in desperation than conscious faith and then the miracle happened. I felt a control and a direction beyond myself—a literal change in my intended way of doing things. Within about ninety seconds my voice had tones of thunder in it and the power and reality of resurrection was declared. I have seldom participated in anything quite like the rest of that funeral service. Its effects were profound; not only were people comforted but they were uplifted by the power of God and the sure knowledge of the triumph of resurrection. It was a felt thing. I went home with joy in my heart for what had happened to others but also with the knowledge of a private miracle and the feeling of the immediacy of God.

This miracle is reminiscent of another of a similar type. Soon after my Baptism in the Spirit I was clearly led of God to start preaching in the open-air. Reference has already been made to this in chapter three. God came again and again in power and many were affected. So great was the interest that hundreds gathered regularly. From an early stage I became aware that God literally strengthened the vocal organs. On one memorable occasion a communist group was on our regular pitch and was rigging up a loud speaker when we arrived. I suggested that we could share the time rather than have two meetings going on close together at the same time. They declined this offer, probably feeling that their loud speaker would give them an advantage. In these days we had no such equipment. Both meetings got under way and in a remarkably short time almost the whole crowd was listening to the gospel. The volume of sound from the human voice seemed to dominate the loudspeaker. Suddenly I began to understand something I had read of the early Methodists. In their day church bells were rung again and again to drown out their preaching— so great was the volume of sound that came from human voices. On this occasion the communists quickly packed up and departed.

Different types of miracles come to mind, and the next one, also associated with open-air work, had a deep and life-long effect upon me.

Over the period that open-airs were held there came times when very real difficulty arose with the police. The site we used was on waste ground but people often stood on a nearby pavement to listen. I always left room between the platform and the pavement for people to come on to the waste ground and moved the platform back as the crowd gathered. The police objected to the pavement being obstructed and I did try to prevent this. I was, however, unwilling to start the meeting so far from the street that people would not be attracted. The controversy went on for a long time, and unless the pavement was actually obstructed the police had no power to stop or forbid the meeting. Against that background a real misunderstanding arose one night. When the pavement was not obstructed the police ordered some young men to move from a little wall on which they were sitting. They were, in fact, listening to the preaching at the time, but evidently prior to the meeting a member of the public had telephoned the police complaining about their behaviour. I immediately suspected that this was a deliberate attempt to break up the gathering, which I knew the police had no legal power to do, and so I intervened in the matter. I was immediately arrested and marched off to jail leaving Mr Cleary, my second in command, to carry on the meeting. I was charged with assaulting the police and obstructing them in carrying out their duties. The first, of course, was totally untrue. The second I can understand.

Now no doubt I had been a thorn in the flesh of the authorities for a long time—having disputed the legalities of the matter with the Chief Constable himself on an earlier occasion. He wanted to impose his will. I wanted what I believed to be the will of God and the two did not seem compatible. The legal right seemed to be on my side. In any case I was now in their hands and they began to use physical violence in the open office. A senior officer shouted to the two officers concerned, 'Don't do it here!' I was taken to a cell where the beating-up continued. I then had a truly miraculous experience. Before the further violence began God presented me with a choice: it seemed that I could either react in a normal human way and defend myself—or put myself entirely into the Hands of God and trust myself to Christ. Immediately I went into Christ. Then things became phenomenal. I seemed to stand outside of myself and observed what was happening to my body as blows rained upon it. I felt no pain at all, but rather a kind of detached interest. I was left lying on the cell floor and still there was no pain. Indeed I only later became aware of where some of the blows had landed, when feeling came back into various parts. For the first time in my life I could understand martyrdom and some of the records of how people reacted. For example, when Blandina had been ripped by a wild cow and pulled out of the arena, she was found to be in a state of ecstasy. So great is the power of God over the body that pain can be blotted out. Now obviously this does not always happen. Many suffer excruciating tortures—but, equally obviously, it sometimes does happen and when it happens it is truly miraculous.

Another very significant thing happened in that cell. In the afterward Satan came and I was sorely tried. It was put to me in an amazingly potent way: suppose evil and not righteousness will ultimately triumph: suppose Satan and not Christ will win in the end, what will you do then? From my point of view, evil was proving to be very strong in that very hour as I lay there on the prison floor—even although Christ had intervened. I cannot easily explain how real the proposition seemed. It was put to me that it might be the followers of a defeated Christ who would endure the agonies of hell through all eternity. What would I do then under the heel of Satan? Would I change allegiance and betray Christ? Suddenly up from my deepest being came the answer. I chose Christ. I could not live without Christ. I wanted to be where He was. I would rather be in hell with Him than anywhere else without Him. At deepest levels, my allegiance to Christ was sealed forever. This has never been undone in my soul. My choice was made not for what I could get from Him—my choice was Christ Himself. I find I cannot live without Him. To have a spirit free in Him is a wonderful thing. When one who has known this is temporarily cut off, it is hell on earth. Having once known the freedom of spirit that is in Him, the bondage that comes with sin is quite intolerable.

I came out of that cell a wiser man. When the case came to court there was no conviction and the officer concerned in the arrest ultimately came to me to put matters right. I appreciated this and should also say that the time came when as a Head Teacher I worked very closely with the police and relations became first-rate!

The last case is one of the most outstanding miracles I have known in the realm of healing and involves the Gault family referred to earlier. My son-in-law's niece, Lisa McAuley, was born with a horrifying array of physical and mental disabilities somewhat resembling the Smith-Lemyli-Opitz Syndrome. She had to lie on her face since she could not swallow her own saliva. She was unable to move herself and it was not expected that she would leave the hospital alive. Yet God gave assurance to each of her parents independently that He would heal her, and this He began to do in stages. First Lisa began to swallow and could be taken home but each feeding time was a two-hour session. When she began to require solid food she was unable to take it. In desperation her mother, Mrs Rosemary McAuley, cried to God that as He had fed the multitudes with the loaves and fishes so would he feed her baby. She then mixed Farex in a saucer and prayed, 'In the Name of Jesus' as each spoonful went into the child's mouth. It took two hours but Lisa never looked back. From that day she ate like any normal child of her age.

And so it was with other disabilities. It seemed that just as the mother reached the end of her tether God would step in miraculously and one more stage of the healing would be accomplished. The most dramatic and humanly inexplicable event in this series of healings was the sudden change in the size of Lisa's brain. Though the doctors had acknowledged surprising physical and mental progress they impressed upon Rosemary that Lisa would never reach full mental capacity because she was microcephalic: her brain was too small. This emphatic statement was made on the occasion of her annual check-up at the Royal Victoria Hospital in Belfast, when Lisa was three-and-a-half years of age. Her mother determined that she would no longer try to convince the doctors of the full extent of Lisa's improvement; if they were to be convinced God would have to show them in His own way.

The following Sunday morning when the family were seated in church, in the quietness that followed the pastor's address on the anointing of the Holy Spirit, Lisa suddenly cried out in such a peculiar way that her mother wondered if she was taking a fit (which she had never done). The child was passed from her little wheelchair along to her mother. As first the father and then the mother touched her it was as though an electric bolt went through them. Still not under-standing, Mrs McAuley asked the child, 'What's the matter?'—'Nuffin!' 'Why are you crying?'—'Not cwyin'!' Then... 'I feel Jesus.'

Later they found out that the pastor, knowing nothing of this conversation, had told his wife that just before Lisa cried out he had looked over and seen the Holy Spirit alight as a dove on her head and then drop to her shoulder.

The following morning brought an unexpected telephone call from the hospital, asking if the parents would mind bringing Lisa for demonstration purposes to a lecture that afternoon. At the conclusion of Professor Nevin's lecture Mrs McAuley asked how he would now rate Lisa's mental condition. The tests were conducted, and he replied that he had no hestitation in describing Lisa's mental condition as normal. Looking him in the eye, and mindful of the previous occasion, the mother asked, 'Professor Nevin, how do you account for this in view of what you told us last week about Lisa's being microcephalic and therefore unable to reach full mental capacity?' She took a note of his reply: 'Mrs McAuley, since your last visit your child's brain has filled out to the size of a normal child's.' Lisa is not yet completely healed but what has happened is truly miraculous. Indeed one doctor used words to the effect that 'Lisa is a miracle child.'[7]

Perhaps I should add, before closing this chaper, that it seems evident from our text, 'to another miracles', that some people are particularly used in the ministry of miracle. I think the gift, at least in its phenomenal operation, is rare. I believe that David Wilkerson has it. I believe that Kathryn Kuhlman had it. But I do not think it is very common. Perhaps as we draw nearer to revival, which the Bible seems so strongly to indicate will flood the land prior to Christ's coming, its incidence may increase. When God draws near in power, miracles certainly do increase, as in Indonesia. I verily believe that days of great interest lie ahead!

Notes

1. Quoted in George Jeffreys, *Pentecostal Rays* (Elim Publishing Co., 1933), p. 195.
2. Fee writes: 'Although Paul would probably include gifts of healings under "workings of miracles," this manifestation most likely covers all other kinds of supernatural activities beyond the healing of the sick' (Fee, *First Epistle to the Corinthians*, p.594).
3. Watchman Nee, *Sit, Walk, Stand* (Victory Press, rev. ed. 1962), pp. 57–64.
4. The writings of Mel Tari refer to some of these matters.
5. I have known the coming of God in revival power and may go into the detail of some of these issues in a later book.
6. A recollection from the late C. E. M. Joad.
7. Lisa's case was of unusual interest to the medical profession. The parents had learned to dread those occasions when they gathered with the specialists round the table to discuss the helpless little child in the middle, since there was always some new problem coming to light. It was on one of these occasions when a vital decision was about to be made by the doctors that Mrs McAuley felt herself lifted above the whole scene into the presence of God. She was startled when He spoke to her: 'And *they* think *they're* the ones making the decisions!' Smiling at the humour of it, she replied, 'That's right, Lord!' Later as they were driving home she had to explain to her puzzled husband why, during a particularly serious part of the discussion, she had been seen smiling and nodding. She believes God gave her that moment of refreshing when He knew how much she needed relief from a heart that was heavy with the daily strain of Lisa's condition. She has even suggested that 'God has an Irish sense of humour!'

7

The Gift of Discernment —and Exorcism

...and to another discernings of spirits (1 Cor 12:10).

I have decided to take the gift of discernment out of sequence. In 1 Corinthians 12:10 the gift of prophecy precedes it, but since prophecy is so closely linked with interpretation and tongues which follow, it seems natural to deal with these three in sequence. I also feel it reasonable to link exorcism with the gift of discernment although exorcism is not specifically referred to in the passage under consideration.

Perhaps I should say first that the gift of discernment has nothing to do with the natural faculty found in so many people whereby they form critical judgments of others.[1] In a church situation the latter propensity can be a curse. The gift on the other hand is a great blessing.

While there are various cases in the Bible where discernment is seen in operation its incidence is not so frequent as is the case with most of the other gifts. One outstanding example is that of Paul and the girl in Philippi who had a spirit of divination (Acts 16). Over a period Paul was disturbed by her shouting after him and his followers:

'These men are servants of the Most High God, which proclaim unto you the way of salvation.' The words she used were true but her activity deeply troubled Paul. One day he turned and cast an evil entity out of her. From that hour her gift of divination departed—much to the dismay of her masters who realised that they could no longer profit financially from her predictions. The Satanic strategy behind the incident may well have been to cause confusion in people's minds over Christianity. Paul would want no impurity in the foundation of the Church. He wanted people to be based on the Word of God and not to have a wrong association with the work of a demon. Satan may also have had a back-up position. When the demon was exorcised the masters of the girl caused a riot. As always in such cases, however, God was glorified in the end. It should be noted that discernment dealt with the spirit which was active in the girl—not with what she said. This is important—for impostors can often become familiar with what is acceptable teaching in Christian circles while being false themselves—and may do much harm if allowed to go on operating. Discernment deals with what they are, with the spirit or spirits under which they operate, rather than just simply with what they say. The evil entities are supernaturally sensed by people with the gift.

The need for this gift is perhaps not always very apparent to Christians until they find themselves in positions of responsibility for others. I was brought up in Christian circles where exorcism was unknown and the work of the Devil was believed in theoretically but little understood in practice. Well do I remember my early days. Even after my own Baptism in the Spirit I came against barrier after barrier in others and knew of the desperate need for the operation of the ministry of exorcism. It was extremely frustrating to meet cases of possession, to know that God could set the sufferers free, to sense their desire to be free and to be able to do nothing about it. Helpful texts just did not seem to work. Endless instruction brought no deliverance. Prayer seemed ineffectual. I found myself faced with a most frustrating impasse—but as in other cases I found that God meets need. I have known a person desperate for the salvation of the souls of his fellows receive the gift of evangelism in an hour of particular need. Driven to desperation we sometimes cast ourselves on God in ways that may unloose His hand in blessing.

For me there came a particular hour. We were gathered for a conference and just prior to the commencement of one session a young man, who had recently been converted, fell screaming to the floor. The people were gathering at the time and my co-leader, who had been involved previously in my reception of spiritual gifts, went to the young man and beckoned me to do likewise. In that hour I believe I received the ministry. There came a great surge of faith and power and the demon fled the scene. The young man was gloriously and completely delivered and was never again troubled by the entity. Today he is a leader in the work of God.

I went on to serve a fairly long apprenticeship. One of my co-leaders, Miss Elizabeth Taylor, has been very deeply used in this ministry. She has not only been able to discern evil entities but in ministering she normally 'sees' them. This has proved to be extremely useful. Often I would not have known whether all were gone from a particular individual or not and she has sometimes said: 'No, there is still another deep down trying to conceal itself,' or something of that kind. There have been three people in our circle who have all had this ability to see. Others of us used in the ministry do not have this particular ability. I tend to sense, rather than see, and I suppose in the end this may produce similar results. Over a period of years I have seen many demons exorcised, and with experience I find the ministry has deepened, but before going on to detail a few sample cases I would like to speak more generally on various aspects of the subject.

The question 'But can a saved person have a demon?' almost always rises in the minds of Christians unfamiliar with exorcism. The answer to this is an unequivocal 'Yes'. Sometimes hands go up in horror—particularly if the saved person referred to has also been baptised in the Spirit. Even so, the answer is still, 'Yes.' The shock of this I can well understand. The very idea of an evil entity within a Christian is repulsive. Indeed many Christians do not even like to think of demons at all—and this is frequently a healthy attitude. But still this does not make demons go away and truth must be faced. When we do turn our minds to the subject and think logically we realise that a person may be truly saved and still be suffering from a horrible physical illness. Within that body which is now a temple of the Holy Spirit a malignant cancer growth can be present. We do not find this impossible to accept. We believe that the day will come when our redemption will be complete. At this point in time the effects of the Fall are evident—but the time will come when 'we shall be changed. For this corruptible must put on incorruption, and this mortal must put on immortality' (1 Cor 15:52–53). But at the moment disease may still be present. In the same way a person may come to Christ and then be baptised in the Spirit while one area or another of personality remains affected by evil power, and as the body needs healing, so other areas can require cleansing from evil which may previously have gained entrance.

Abundant evidence has come over recent years that many people, both saved and baptised in the Spirit, have discovered that deliverance has still been necessary and again and again it has been received. This has applied not only to young and inexperienced Christians but also to leaders in the work of God. I noticed in the writings of Don Basham that as a mature leader he had become aware that debilitating fear which gripped and almost paralysed him from time to time was caused by an evil power. This had gained entrance when, as a child, he had been exposed to a 'horror' film. The demon was cast out and he was set totally free. He indicated that Derek Prince had also, as a mature Christian, realised that he had a particularly bad temper which had a demon connection. He required and received deliverance.[2] Let such cases encourage the rest of us, and if you find that you do need deliverance in particular areas come with anticipation rather than with terror, and also recognise that while you may desire deliverance, there can be that within you which cannot help feeling terror.

A second question arises: 'How do the evil spirits initially gain entrance?' This opens up a fascinating area. Quite simply sin frequently provides the openings. There are many types of sin and there are many types of demon. When sin is indulged in there is very real danger that demons will find an entrance through, for example, lust, sexual deviation, over-indulgence in alcohol, tobacco, drug addiction, an ungoverned temper, jealousy, greed. In addition to entrance resulting from positive sin, it seems that entities also take advantage of areas of weakness to gain footholds. For example, a sudden terror can leave a spirit of fear behind it. Accidents can sometimes have the same effect. Sorrow too long indulged or which is allowed to go too deep can open the personality unhappily to demon foothold. Deep control of the human personality is ever necessary. We should never wrongly or excessively indulge our emotions lest in so doing we provide highways for the entrance of the enemy.

I would next like to draw attention to Christ and His ministry in this realm. About twenty-five percent of His recorded ministry was related to exorcism. It is amazing that One so gentle and kindly only had to move into a locality for the demons to manifest themselves and cry out. They could not stand His presence. 'What have we to do with thee, thou Son of God? art thou come hither to torment us...?' (Mt 8:29) I suppose His presence spelled hell for them. I have noticed that demons often do recognise people in whom the Holy Spirit is manifestly present—particularly people with a ministry of exorcism. Demons can become quite agitated in the presence of such people. Christians generally, however, can pass in and out of localities without provoking the kind of reaction which Christ met.

Notice too that Christ taught that before dealing with the 'strong man's' goods the 'strong man' should first be bound. This He Himself did. Again and again he dealt with the demons in an area and then proceeded to work the works of God. We should do the same, and indeed we sometimes have to do just that. At times Christ cast out single demons, it could be of dumbness, blindness or sickness but on one very instructive occasion he cast out 'Legion'. In the man who dwelt in the tombs, whom no man could bind, there were evil entities. 'My name,' he said, 'is Legion, for we are many.' Frequently, in our day, similar situations are met and those involved in the ministry should not too readily think that all is over when one or two demons have revealed themselves and been cast out. They should hold themselves open to deal with 'Legion' if necessary, and sometimes this involves a number of sessions. There are times when an individual might not be able to stand more than a certain measure of deliverance at one sitting. The physical body might not be able to survive it.[3]

Note that Christ gave the Seventy power over demons and generally they were able to cast these out. On one occasion, however, they came on a case which they were not able to deal with and Christ said, 'This kind can come out by nothing save prayer and fasting' (Mk 9:29). From this we should learn a lesson. There are different types of demon. They have different degrees of power. They do not all come out in the same way. Some cases require greater preparation on the part of the person ministering than do others. We should dwell deeply in God and sensitively obey the leading of the Spirit. It was Christ Who commissioned the Seventy. It is He Who gives power over all the power of the enemy.

From time to time people who do not know Christ may try to use His Name. This is a very dangerous thing to do. Indeed this is a realm into which no man should try to go, who is not definitely taken there by God. In the Book of Acts we read of the seven sons of Sceva who tried to exorcise in the name of Christ and the man in whom the demon dwelt leaped on them saying, 'Jesus I know, and Paul I know; but who are ye?' and they fled naked. Again let me warn—do not go into this realm carelessly or experimentally. Be led of God. If He takes you in to it He will provide your covering. Never go beyond that covering. In that realm you deal with real power. 'It is the anointing that breaks the yoke.' *You* never can. Amazingly God tunes His servants for this ministry. I often see and hear things which in my early days might have had a seriously disturbing psychological effect, whose consequences could have been permanent. Nowadays as I observe from a position of cover, I may see a body writhe and twist; I may hear screams of fearful horror; I may witness convulsions so severe that the person concerned fears that he will die; and through all this I may remain quite unmoved. Compassionate towards the person—yes!—but with the iron of God towards the demons. I can be unaffected by all their performances. Demons like to deal in fear. Perfect love has no place for fear. God's servants can and should be wholly covered. I also find that I do not become at all personally involved with the demons. I am a channel for God. I leave Him to deal with them.

There are a number of points of interest I have learned over the years. Demons have supernatural knowledge. On one occasion a man who was tormented heard that I was coming to his area. We had never met but evidently on receiving this information, something turned over inside him—he was about a hundred miles distant from me at the time. The demon knew of its danger. The man had no idea at that time, so far as I know, that he had a demon. When the meeting took place—down he went on the floor and a demon was dealt with. On a second occasion I was conscious that one individual in a company had a demon. The circumstances were such that I could not easily arrange a time for ministry—but it occurred to me to isolate the person from the company and have them travel in my car. They had no knowledge of what I had in mind until the demon within them reacted. The arrangement was carried through and the demon exorcised.

It is important to realise that, as in Christ's day, demons also speak, often through the lips of people in whom they have their dwelling. Apparently they can speak directly to the sufferer—they speak temptingly, insinuatingly, providing ideas and concealing their own presence and part. Frequently they give fearful threats of dire trouble and even death when the sufferer seeks deliverance. They can become extremely agitated and cause real fear. I remember one man who was desperately afflicted. He suffered from unnatural lust but had been converted and faced a terrible situation. He came for ministry but told us even as he sat in the vestry that he was being told inside himself not to go on with this. He would die if he did. In spite of our reassurances he ultimately gave way to terror and rose and literally ran out of the church and never reappeared. Demon threatenings are very frequent but some people reach the stage where they are so desperate to be free that they refuse to believe the lying voices and go through with exorcism.

Amongst very recent cases with which I have had to deal were those of two brothers. The first came to a shattering experience in life with the death of a little daughter of five from an incurable type of leukaemia. He was very deep in sin of many kinds and was a slave to alcohol but he loved that child. He had a Roman Catholic background and had no doubt that she had gone to be with Christ and he knew that in his condition he could never join her. Immediately he began to seek Christ and ultimately came into one of our services. At an early stage he told me of his drink problem and on being prayed for was instantly delivered from both alcohol and tobacco. He never smoked or touched a drop again. At this point he was still unsaved. A week or two passed and one Monday night I drew him aside to broach the subject of conversion. As it happened he had already decided that he wanted to be converted, but he realised that he had been running his business on dishonest lines and that this would have to be dealt with if he was to live a Christian life. That night he had his books in his car to take to his accountant in the morning, having decided to go straight from that hour. He intended to seek salvation on the Tuesday night. When I learned of the position I said, 'Why not tonight, Raymond? God knows your attitude and will receive you.' We bowed together and he found Christ right there. I then laid hands on him and he was gloriously baptised in the Holy Spirit.[4]

Again a period passed. Raymond found himself very close to God and things were progressing well. Then came another Monday night and a part in the Bible Study alerted him to the fact that there was something wrong inside. Amongst other things I had spoken of certain types of sin, of demon entrance and exorcism and he was evidently deeply disturbed. I had no suspicion that he had any kind of demon trouble at that point. A very miserable time ensued

117

for him but he came on the Saturday night following saying he feared he had a demon. Now many people after hearing about exorcism get such an idea when, in fact, they are not really affected. I still had no reason to think that there was anything wrong but said: 'Well, we'll soon see. We'll go to the vestry.' I dealt first that night with another young man who did require, and who received, deliverance. Then Raymond came in. I laid hands on him and in a very short time he had what he has described as 'a series of screaming convulsions.' He actually feared he would die, but he allowed the ministry to continue. There were probably about seven waves. Over a period there was further ministry until finally there came a point where he was himself instructed to take power over the power of the enemy and he now knows total freedom.

Raymond is a soul winner and very soon his brother found Christ. Edward went on for a time, then deeply backslid and came deeply under the power of alcohol. It ruined his business and his home. In due time he turned to Raymond who in turn brought him for prayer, suspecting the need for deliverance. This he received powerfully. I think he too wondered if he might die—quite a number do wonder this. But a man is totally safe on the operating table of God with the Divine Physician at work. Edward lived all right to proclaim the greatness of God, and he too is now totally free from alcohol.

Now even if either of these two men should have a collapse—for we are human and in the body—the reality of the miracles remains. Demons have been driven out. But I always remember what one man of God said: 'I can cast demons out—but I know of no way of keeping them out if the person concerned lives carelessly.'

Demons not only speak to the persons in whom they dwell, they also speak through them—sometimes to others generally and frequently to the person or persons involved in exorcism. It is vital for such persons to distinguish between the voice of the person concerned and that of the indwelling demon or demons. Confusion on this can cause real problems. On the first occasion on which I noticed this, the voice shouted, 'No, no, no!' as exorcism was in progress. I thought that the person was resisting the ministry and only later realised that it was the demon which was resisting its own expulsion. This kind of thing I have found happen frequently. Undue attention should never be paid to what demons say. The person ministering should be deep in God and receive his urgings and direction from Him alone. It is not good to be distracted by evil manifestations. I have known a person come for ministry but when it came to the point try to evade prayer by endless talking and ultimately fall to the ground shouting for Satan to come to his assistance. Act for the person and ignore the demon.

A number of years ago one of my friends, the Rev. John Anderson, used to minister in Glasgow and he spoke of a very interesting case of demons speaking. John had been for some time in charge of an assembly but felt that his ministry was deficient and sought God with fasting and prayer. When the waiting time was over he took his first meeting and at the end of it when he called people forward for ministry a woman came out. She was the illegitimate daughter of a medium and was deeply possessed. John prayed for her and she went down on the floor. Ultimately she was taken to a side room and covered with a blanket while John and other elders continued to pray. The noise became so bad that they decided to go out to the country. As it happened the field where they chose to continue to minister was one in which the murderer, Manuel, had shortly before buried one of his victims. John did not know this. As he continued to minister things became very grim. Evidently the elders could not stand any more and departed. Suddenly there came a change. John felt an anointing come upon him and immediately the defiant attitude of the demons altered. It is probable that at that moment he received the ministry of exorcism. Instead of screams of defiance the demons became ingratiating: 'We have never done you any harm. Just leave us alone.' They began to plead—but John would have none of it. He cast them out and the woman was set totally free. Then the Holy Spirit fell on her and she began to sing that beautiful hymn, 'I'd rather have Jesus than anything this world affords today...' As she sang she was baptised in the Spirit. By this time the police had arrived. The noise had evidently been very great. There was John alone with the woman. 'Who are you?' said a policeman, no doubt remembering the Manuel business. 'A Pentecostal preacher,' said John. 'You don't look like one,' said the officer. By this time both John's jacket and tie were off (as frequently happened when he got involved in his work). John went to put an arm on the shoulder of one of the officers. 'Don't touch me,' the man said, jumping back. 'I saw what happened to that woman when you put your hands on her.' Presumably he feared the action of God.

On another occasion a big woman came forward and said to John, who was a little man: 'Why should a big woman like me be afraid of a wee man like you?' and then she spat in his eye. Graciously and forgivingly he wiped his eye, whereupon she spat in his other eye. Warfare then commenced and the woman fell to the floor. I presume she was set free as so many others were, but the close detail of the case I no longer accurately recollect. At times the demon will threaten the life of the person used of God. I have known several cases of this—but in no case has the person drawn back—and death has not occurred. The threat, however, can be very real. With this ministry God gives a tremendous strength and determination. Something of His own iron comes into His children.

Apart from threats directly made by demons, people

used in this ministry have to walk carefully. The ministry is much opposed by the kingdom of darkness and the people concerned can be unusually assaulted. In the case of one who was something of a pioneer, I know that evil powers pursued over a long period before the ministry commenced. It seems also that Satan himself, as distinct from his emissaries, sometimes takes the field. When this happens things are always serious. Sometimes Christ too seems to come in a particular way. In a case I was dealing with recently I really reached the end of my tether. In the very midst of being ministered to, the person turned and indicated that things were worsening. A tremendous desire was rising to plunge right into the very sin which had caused the demon entry in the first place. I did not know what to do. To continue might make things worse. I paused, but did not remove my hand. (Unlike some others I often lay hands on people with demons.) Suddenly Christ came and I said, 'I have no more to do with this case. Christ Himself is here.' What a commotion there was. The demons recognised the new situation and could no longer remain.

Perhaps I should also mention the tremendous exhilaration and joy that is associated with this ministry. Salvation brings a great happiness; healings have a flavour of their own—a warm contentment; Baptisms in the Spirit for me have a robust joy; but again and again with exorcism I feel almost an ecstasy of triumph. My soul shouts, 'Hallelujah!' This is a word which I do not frequently use, and never casually, but again and again at the moment when the battle goes against the demons and I feel them move, the word comes out in great joy and power. When they have gone I feel the triumph of Christ. His lordship is so wonderfully demonstrated.

People sometimes ask where demons go when they are cast out. I do not always know. Sometimes they are instructed to go to the pit but not always. In Scripture in one case they begged Christ to allow them to go into swine and permission was granted. Some have wondered at this—but it was not a very permanent home they found. Christ knew that the swine would drown. Some again might say: 'What about the owners of the swine and the swine themselves?' If you study the laws of Israel you may come to the conclusion that the Gadarenes should not have been keeping swine in the first place.

I am reminded of my friend John Anderson again. On one occasion he was addressing a company in which a number of ministers were present. A demon-possessed woman rushed on to the platform and dropped at his feet. Looking at his watch he said to the congregation, 'In one minute from now this demon is coming out—but where will it go? Are you all right? Is there any covered sin that you are not bringing out? Will you be quite safe?' Suddenly one of the company clung to the platform rail seeking God for mercy. The demon did come out but not before John used the occasion to indicate the danger of living carelessly close to the field of exorcism.

I would also draw attention to the warning Christ gave regarding the position of a person from whom an evil spirit has gone. The person should have the empty place filled with God lest the departed entity return with others and re-enter — 'the last state of that man becometh worse than the first' (Mt 12:45).

I have already indicated that demons are of various types. Amongst the most common are those associated with the sins of lust, sexual deviation, over-indulgence in alcohol, tobacco, drug addiction, an ungoverned temper, jealousy and greed. To these we can add witchcraft, murder, suicide, pride, anger and hatred. The list is very long. Scores of types have been identified. There has also been much speculation about their origins—some regard them as fallen angels—but the truth is that Scripture has given little indication on the point. They are regarded in the Bible as servants of Satan, as part of his kingdom, operating under his power. Often they name themselves or are at least identified during exorcism. If they have not identified themselves, when the person used in exorcism comes on their names, there is often violent reaction in the person being prayed for. The demons seem to suffer agony during exorcism.

The value of the ability to see the entities will be obvious to readers. In the last chapter on miracles I mentioned that the Rev. Duncan Campbell literally saw demons depart from a meeting hall. Twice in my own life I too have seen demons: once many years ago and the case was very horrible. The demon was one of sickness and it had been attacking a child of God without his knowing of its existence. In an unusual moment it became visible as it was being cast out. Such a sight one does not forget. Very recently at a time when trouble was threatening I awoke and in those moments between sleeping and waking which I have found significant throughout a lifetime[5] I suddenly saw and recognised a demon which immediately departed. I have not, however, been given the ability to trace demon movement visually when I am used in exorcism as some others in our fellowship have.

In one of our early cases this was very marked and effective. The gentleman who was receiving ministry was deeply tormented. The physical manifestations as the demons were dealt with were horrific and the sound was great. After about fifteen had gone, each visually seen, in snake form, it seemed that the exorcism was over, but then came the warning: 'No, there is one left. It is old and has been in the body for a long time. It is deep down in the personality and thinks it is concealed. It is very strong.' After a great struggle this too came out and the man was totally free. The visual side had proved critical.

In a more recent case when another person was ministering along with me a young man came for deliverance, indicating to me the sin which had caused the condition. He was prayed for and immediately there was a clearance—but again I was warned: 'They are not all out. It is as though a glass with dirty water has been emptied but a sediment remains on the bottom. If this is not cleared and the glass fills up, in time the water will again be polluted.' I continued to minister and evidently it appeared visually that all the sediment came out as though attached to a string. The young man was set free. Notes of what was actually seen were taken at the time and these read as follows:

> ...a vessel containing a dark brown colloidal solution. During first stage it was swirled round and was emptied out. By this point there was a measure of cleansing but as clean water poured in a sticky sediment remained at the bottom. There came the knowledge that unless this too was expelled the water would continue to become muddy and polluted.
>
> During the second stage the sediment itself was disturbed until ultimately it began to be peeled away from the bottom of the vessel. Once it started coming away, it wasn't long until it was only attached at one small point. Ultimately this last part was detached and the sediment was flushed out.

Again and again I have seen these ministries in operation and can testify to their tremendous usefulness. The fact that I lack the visual side may have helped develop a spiritual sensitivity for *feeling* if demons have all gone or not. Having worked with people with the ability to see I certainly know of the value of the gift. There is a sense in which these people are truly seers—they do see. I have noticed that some of the visual imagery which is given is remarkably clear and is often colourful. Demons may sometimes be seen as buzzing bees, or they may be snake-like in form. The pictures are very varied but always remarkably relevant to the condition being dealt with. The following examples will illustrate the point: 'This one is coming out like a barbed fish—moving backwards. It is rending as it comes. This is very painful.' The person was dealt with very tenderly afterwards—until the healing oil of God came upon him. He was totally delivered and went on to be much used of God. In another case demons were described as contaminating the whole bloodstream—so deep was the pollution.

Notes taken of the visual side of a few more cases may be of interest to readers. In the following case the young man was set free:

> ...insubstantial yet oppressive slate grey cloud, billowing and swirling. By its nature difficult to get a hold of. Gradually it was made to disperse. It thinned until only a few small wisps remained. These were more stubborn and subtle but ultimately vanished as the intensity increased.
>
> While ministering in the afterward for an infilling there came the knowledge that God was minded to use the life. He was part of the harvest field spoken of but the cloud had prevented the sun from ripening the crop/fruit.

In the next case again a young man was set free—this time from a demon connected with smoking:

> ...just a darkness, a seeming nothingness, too thick to pierce. Then the true situation was revealed—one very small, though strong, demon was putting out this dark substance to screen itself. It wanted to remain hidden because it knew if detected, it would have to go. Several times it succeeded in this, evading the inevitable, but ultimately its ability to emit darkness was lost. When this happened it swirled and slithered around a bit—still difficult to pin down. As it came out it did so angrily and reluctantly.

One day a Christian father brought his son for help. He feared that he was in need of deliverance. It was discerned that in this case demons had not in fact gained entrance although they were seeking it and the danger was very real. The visual imagery was interesting:

> ...external, not internal. Small creatures circling the being, hands joined as in a dance. When challenged they ultimately broke up but remained within close enough vicinity to strike again if foolish behaviour is engaged in.

The position was described and warning given—but in this case I fear that foolish behaviour was engaged in again.

The next case concerned a very fine young man who was sincerely endeavouring to follow Christ and was often assaulted by evil. The notes read:

> ...external, not internal. A dark stickiness which was resistant to all human effort. The moment it was removed from one part of the body, it stuck fast to that part used in its removal. Only when the blood of Christ was applied did it dissolve—this was the only antidote—the only solution.

The final case I want to instance was very sad. It relates to a deeply depressed man who was not set free. The notes read:

> ...a cube-shaped box with many nails holding the lid down. Much time had obviously passed since the nails first went in, as they were rusty and were almost indistinguishable from the box itself. There was no sense of them beginning to be turned or be loosed. As a result of the lid being fastened darkness (depression) was trapped in the inside.

I have noticed that young children can be affected and it is with some indignation that I write this. The indignation is at Satan. He is so cruel. Never in dealing with exorcism allow yourself any softness or consideration where he is concerned. We should be implacable against him in God. He forever seeks to destroy, and infants are not immune. One little child suffered horrible nightmares (this is often connected with demon activity) and his parents sought ministry. As the child was approached the demon fled and he was never troubled again. The people of God ought to seek deliverance. We do not have to endure this tyranny of evil and very often deliverance is very quick. Nor are all exorcisms either sensational or horrific. Under anointed preaching demons may often leave people with neither outward manifestations nor as a result of special ministry. In other cases there may be little more than a cough. Sometimes with more drastic cases there may be nausea and vomiting. Sometimes there is horrible screaming and writhing, *but in all cases God is to be trusted and the consequences are always well worth the cure.*

Often it is wise to minister privately. First, the sufferer may wish his affairs to remain under the seal of the confessional and, secondly, the manifestations of evil through him as the demons resist God may be very frightening to others. Thirdly, the iron which becomes evident in the servant of God with its reflection in his voice can also alarm the faint-hearted. This picture is not really like the conception of a meek and mild Saviour which many people have. It reminds rather of the stern and powerful aspects of the character of God.

It is not, however, always possible to minister privately. Sometimes, as in the ministry of Christ, demons call out in public gatherings and people go down one after another. In such circumstances I would normally minister on the spot and I have found that God gives His own covering to the company. Indeed I have known a company come under tremendous power in such a moment and share wonderfully in the ultimate triumph of exorcism. There is no hard and fast rule.

I find in writing of exorcism, it is somewhat like writing of Baptism in the Spirit. The cases are far too numerous to include them all and yet each has its own peculiar features and interest. I have never become used to miracle. I am never casual about the actions of God—but I cannot attempt in one short chapter to cover the whole field. Sadly, the cases multiply. In recent days far more young people have been deeply affected by evil power before they come to Christ than was the case twenty years ago. We live in a permissive society when television can at times be like an open sewer pouring its filth right into our living-rooms. Pornography is deeply demon-connected and is ever increasing. Ordinary newspapers are dredging up filth from the gutters of human activity and standards are falling disastrously. Men and women of real Christian character are sometimes shocked at how they themseves have come to accept that such things have become part of life in the twentieth century. While they do not condone, they realise that where once they would have been deeply shocked, they now scarcely react to the revelation of some new horror. I was a Head Teacher for many years and witnessed the steady decline. The advent of video has now made things much worse. Young people often now choose the horror and obscene films—films of violence and perversion. They soak themselves in evil. Is it any wonder that if and when they come to Christ they are in deep need of exorcism? The corollary is that the church is in deep need of more people to operate in this field. Have you a thought for Zion's condition and Zion's need? Is there an answer within you—'Here am I: send me'? Do not enter this realm lightly—but prayerfully explore the ground and listen to the voice of God.

Some may wonder if there can be indications of demon possession or of demon activity within an individual, which a person without the gift of discernment may perceive. There are, in fact, sometimes irrational habits which indicate the condition, for example, a particular pleasure in illtreating animals; an unusual cruelty; a fascination for dirty things which normal people find repulsive. I remember a pupil once took an unusual delight in inflicting pain. He turned to Christ and very quickly a demon was expelled. It is dangerous, however, to go looking for demons under every stone or to blame demons for sins which fallen human nature is quite capable of committing without any assistance from Satan. Demons are real and responsible for much—but human nature is weak and we are ourselves responsible for many of our own sins. Recognise that there are demons and that they are active but do not over-emphasise this or become morbid about it. Approach cases in a straightforward way and do not assume demon presence until you have reason to do so.

Distinguish also between full demon possession and various degrees of demon activity within an individual. There can be tormenting from outside. There can be a foothold in one or more areas. The grip can be light or strong—the manifestation infrequent or frequent. Left undisturbed the demon will seek to extend its grip and go for vital areas, for example, the mind—the area where imagination holds sway. Lust will go for feeling parts of the personality and move strongly to the mind. All must be guarded, and for all God's children there is victory in Him.

Perhaps I may relate three more incidents before closing. I once had a telephone call from a doctor of medicine whom I had never met but who knew friends of mine very well. She arranged to see me and it transpired that she had been subjected to a truly horrific psychic experience in earlier years. Evil really had appeared to her and she feared that there was a demon within her to be dealt with. I arranged for my co-leader to minister in this case and indeed in the moment when the two came within seeing distance of each other, the demon in one challenged God in the other. This happened in the open street and we adjourned to the church where there was a wonderful and permanent deliverance.

The next case made an indelible impression on me. A young university student from the Far East began to attend services. He had a Buddhist background but had become interested in Christianity. Gradually he passed from being merely interested in, to being deeply affected by, the services. A point came where he could no longer stand upright in a particular gathering and he had to be helped into an ante-room where it became evident that he was deeply possessed. The wicked spirit was very strong and it ultimately came screaming out through a mouth which seemed to be fixed open to an incredible extent. It was a complete and wonderful deliverance. That young man is today standing for God in very difficult circumstances in a very dark land. Several times in this chapter I have referred to my co-leader who has been so deeply used in this ministry. She took the initiative in this case. She seems to have the ability to sense forces of darkness in distant foreign fields. In one case she did this accurately in ministering to a missionary home on furlough from the Near East.[6] In another she dealt with what I suppose were ancestral spirits troubling a man of God. He had eastern blood and it appeared that something had carried over to him from earlier generations. Satan attempted to take his life but was totally thwarted. The man was completely set free and he is today a leader amongst God's people. Another interesting facet of this ministry is an ability to sense the presence of a major evil power—such as one which may hold sway over a whole city—as distinct from comparatively minor entities of evil.[7]

The final case is one of the earliest in which I was involved and the background is particularly significant. Indeed it had a lifelong effect on me. I was due to take a house meeting in Gorebridge, south of Edinburgh, on the occasion concerned. I arrived in good time and was alone in one apartment preparing for preaching when suddenly God drew near and began to give particular revelation. Now I have learned that when God does this we should never interrupt the process. We may stop it but we cannot restart it. It behoves us to listen quietly. For years I had been preaching the gospel— presenting Christ to the world— seeking to show that He was the Son of God and that salvation might be had in His Name. Suddenly it was revealed to me that much of my address had been to the minds of men. I wanted to change their thinking. I wanted them to understand that Jesus was the Son of God—that He died for their sins, that they should believe this. I wanted them to give up all false belief and have a right under-standing of truth. This was all good but suddenly God showed me that He was not interested in the minds of men only. He is interested in the whole being and personality of man and he desires to meet men at every level of human need.

I saw a wholeness in the gospel I had never seen before. The revelation was very clear and very powerful. In due time I went next door to preach. I was full of what God had shown me and I preached it. At the end, I asked if there was anyone present who had a need that they wanted God to meet that night. One lady raised her hand. I had been aware of this lady before, with an undefined feeling that there was something just a little strange there—although even that is perhaps putting it too strongly and may contain an element of wisdom after the event. I went to her and spoke. She indicated that again and again she got to a particular place in meetings or in prayer and then met a barrier and could get no further. 'It is like a ball hitting the ceiling;' she said, 'it can never go any higher but bounces back again.' I prayed, and suddenly there was a horrible scream and her face twisted. I was still very new to exorcism but I persisted. In a moment the entity was gone and she was wonderfully baptised in the Spirit—singing most sweetly in new tongues as the Spirit gave her utterance. She said later that she had been in her former condition from comparatively early years. We all rejoiced greatly. (Many of the company had just received their Pentecost.) There was no recurrence of the trouble. I have never forgotten the desire and ability of God to meet need at every level of human personality—mind, soul and body—and through the years I have regularly preached this and seen God honour His word.

I feel there is so much left unsaid. Memories flit in and out—in one case, of the departing demon or demons shouting at me that they would be back (and indeed they did come back since the person returned to the sin which had caused the infection). But thank God they were expelled again and at the time of writing the person is free. Again and again I have noticed physical reaction in a person with demons when the subject was mentioned—reactions that they could not control. Another area of interest relates to the question of whether sufferers ought always to be prayed for when affected. I have found that if they are not keen to be delivered it is an uphill battle. If they are not prepared to renounce the sin which has caused the condition they are perhaps better not to be prayed for at all—save that they will come to a better frame of mind. Even if they say they have renounced the sin and truly want deliverance, care should be exercised. The only safe way is to go with God. I was shocked to discover from one individual that while there can be pain with exorcism there can also be a certain carnal attraction. Old scenes revive, and the memories of past sins connected with the possession may come again strongly. The individual may wallow in these memories instead of renouncing them and being delivered. If this happens the person can plunge back into the mire. It is indeed a glorious ministry but the dangers too are very real.

I end this chapter by giving glory to God for all I have seen Him do in this realm, for all that He is, for the glory of the moments when I have known 'the heel of Christ' tread 'on the head of the serpent'. I rejoice in His on-going triumph.

Notes

[1] While Fee recognises the phenomenon of testing spirits, he also associates this gift (mistakenly, in my view) with the discerning of prophecy, as in 1 Corinthians 14. See his *First Epistle to the Corinthians*, p.596.

[2] Don Basham, *Deliver us from Evil* (Hodder and Stoughton, 1973).

[3] See the case of Doreen Irvine as recorded in her book *From Witchcraft to Christ* (Concordia Publishing House, 1973).

[4] In earlier days, I used to prepare people over a long period for the Baptism in the Spirit and in these days Baptisms tended to be few and far between. More recently I find myself expecting Baptism to come soon after conversion. I remember one case where I had been invited to speak to an interdenominational group. The invitation came some months before the event and I was given a clear-cut subject. The night to speak arrived and to my consternation I had completely forgotten the word. I could substitute no other. Fortunately, minutes before the meeting was due to commence, it came back. I preached on revival and a movement of the Spirit started in the group and ultimately about thirty people were baptised in the Spirit. There came a point where one remained unmet. He was a mature man who had been deep in sin and was still unsaved. The hour came when he was desperate for salvation and at 10.45 one Sunday night the telephone rang and I was asked to go to help him. It was, as it generally is, easy to point a genuinely seeking soul to Christ. He received quickly and gladly, and I was about to go with him to share the rejoicing with the other members of the family but I was restrained. I thought: 'Why not pray for his Baptism as well?' I explained to him briefly that the Spirit Who had brought Christ to him in saving power, wanted to come right into his body and take possession of him. We prayed and then I was truly shocked. His face twisted as though in agony. So soon after sensing such joy I was witnessing real anguish. I thought, 'What would my non-Pentecostal Christian acquaintances say now if they could see this?' To cause a new convert such distress! This seemed a terrible thing! I clung to God and suddenly there came a change. Light broke upon him and he began to praise God in beautiful

133

and fluent new tongues. He told me afterwards that as I began to pray he felt as though he was being torn apart inside. The truth is that God had saved his soul a few minutes earlier. He had been saved from the penalty of sin. But the inner grip of sin had not broken. As God came to baptise there was a thorough probing to the roots, and the power of sin was broken. Note that as with Cornelius and his household the Baptism followed conversion very closely.

On another occasion four of my pupils were present at a church service and expressed an interest in Salvation at the end of the meeting. I took them to the vestry and even as I explained Salvation the Spirit fell and three of them were baptised on the spot.

If our meetings are in the power and demonstration of the Holy Spirit this kind of event should be a regular occurrence.

[5] God often has particular access to his children at such a time. The usual barriers and defences are not in place.

[6] Donald McPhail — 'Little Donald' of Lewis Revival fame.

[7] See the story of Daniel being opposed by the prince of the kingdom of Persia (Dan 10:13).

8

The Gift of Tongues[1]

... to another divers kinds of tongues (1 Cor 12:10).

The number of references in Scripture to tongues is so limited that in a study of the subject it seems wise to list these at the outset.

There is only one from the Old Testament and this is also quoted in the New Testament:

Nay, but by men of strange lips and with another tongue will he speak to this people (Is 28:11).

Paul in referring to this writes:

In the law it is written, By men of strange tongues and by the lips of strangers will I speak unto this people; and not even thus will they hear me, saith the Lord (1 Cor 14:21).

Had Paul not precisely identified the Isaiah reference with 'tongues' we would very possibly have interpreted this verse otherwise. When we come to the New Testament we read that Christ said to his disciples:

And these signs shall follow them that believe: in my name shall they cast out devils: they shall speak with new tongues (Mk 16:17).

In a description of events on the day of Pentecost we read:

And there appeared unto them tongues parting asunder, like as of fire; and it sat upon each one of them. And they were all filled with the Holy Spirit, and began to speak with other tongues, as the Spirit gave them utterance (Acts 2:3–4).

In connection with the receiving of the Spirit by Cornelius and his household we read:

And they of the circumcision which believed were amazed, as many as came with Peter, because that on the Gentiles also was poured out the gift of the Holy Ghost. For they heard them speak with tongues, and magnify God (Acts 10:45–46).

In the case of the Ephesian twelve we read:

And when Paul had laid his hands upon them, the Holy Ghost came on them; and they spake with tongues, and prophesied' (Acts 19:6).

In listing gifts of the Spirit Paul wrote:

. . . to another [is given] divers kinds of tongues; and to another the interpretation of tongues (1 Cor 12:10).

He continued:

And God hath set some in the church, first apostles, secondly prophets, thirdly teachers, then miracles, then gifts of healings, helps, governments, divers kinds of tongues (1 Cor 12:28).

. . . Have all gifts of healings? Do all speak in tongues? Do all interpret? (1 Cor 12:30).

136

If I speak with the tongues of men and of angels, but have not love, I am become sounding brass, or a clanging cymbal (1 Cor 13:1).

Love never faileth: but whether there be prophecies, they shall be done away; whether there be tongues, they shall cease; whether there be knowledge, it shall be done away (1 Cor 13:8).

In giving some explanation of tongues and in advising on their proper use Paul continued:

For he that speaketh in a tongue speaketh not unto men, but unto God; for no man understandeth; but in the spirit he speaketh mysteries (1 Cor 14:2).

He that speaketh in a tongue edifieth himself; but he that prophesieth edifieth the church. Now I would have you all speak with tongues, but rather that ye should prophesy: and greater is he that prophesieth than he that speaketh with tongues, except he interpret, that the church may receive edifying. But now, brethren, if I come unto you speaking with tongues, what shall I profit you, unless I speak to you either by way of revelation, or of knowledge, or of prophesying, or of teaching? (1 Cor 14:4–6).

Wherefore let him that speaketh in a tongue pray that he may interpret. For if I pray in a tongue, my spirit prayeth, but my understanding is unfruitful. What is it then? I will pray with the spirit [which in this context means 'tongues'], and I will pray with the understanding also: I will sing with the spirit [tongues], and I will sing with the understanding also. Else if thou bless with the spirit, how shall he that filleth the place of the unlearned say the Amen at thy giving of thanks, seeing he knoweth not what thou sayest? For thou verily givest thanks well, but the other is not edified. I thank God, I speak with tongues more than you all: howbeit in the church I had rather speak five words with my understanding, that I might instruct others also, than ten thousand words in a tongue (1 Cor 14:13–19).

Next comes the reference to Isaiah 28:11 already mentioned and clear identification of this with tongues is seen in the following passages:

> Wherefore tongues are for a sign, not to them that believe, but to the unbelieving.... If therefore the whole church be assembled together, and all speak with tongues, and there come in men unlearned or unbelieving, will they not say that ye are mad? (1 Cor 14:22–23).

Paul gives further instruction in the following verses:

> What is it then, brethren? When ye come together, each one hath a psalm, hath a teaching, hath a revelation, hath a tongue, hath an interpretation. Let all things be done unto edifying. If any man speaketh in a tongue, let it be by two, or at the most three, and that in turn; and let one interpret: but if there be no interpreter, let him keep silence in the church; and let him speak to himself, and to God (1 Cor 14:26–28).

> Wherefore, my brethren, desire earnestly to prophesy, and forbid not to speak with tongues. But let all things be done decently and in order (1 Cor 14:39–40.

The first question that is likely to arise in the mind of readers unfamiliar with the subject is simply: What are tongues? Basically they are utterances through human lips of words which are unintelligible to the person uttering them.[2] This answer, however, merely deepens the mystery. Does that mean, you may say, that a person speaks words which to him have no meaning? The answer is 'yes'. Immediately you ask: 'How does he do it? And what is the purpose of doing it?'

When a person is in control of his faculties and he commences to speak in a normal way, the tongue is under his own control. He speaks the words which rise in his mind and these are meaningful and significant—not only to himself but to all others who are familiar with the language in which he is speaking. The vital point is that he is himself in control of the operation. There are times, however, when he may feel an inadequacy in his own language; e.g., feelings can run so strong that he may say, 'I just can't find words to express this emotion.' Secondly, in prayer the use of words sometimes takes the person praying down sidelines and instead of concentrating on the main burden the mind is distracted and wanders as word associations arise.

When a person speaks in tongues, as on the day of Pentecost, he is not under his own control, but comes under the control of the Holy Spirit. The organs of speech are still the normal organs of speech but the motivating power is no longer human but Divine. The Holy Spirit comes upon the human spirit and takes control.[3] We do not read in Scripture that the Spirit speaks in tongues. The person upon whom He comes does the speaking, but it is the Spirit who gives the power. Thus basically with speaking in tongues there is a change of control. When this happens the language used, while unknown to the speaker, may be quite familiar to others as, for example, on the day of Pentecost when many languages were recognised by Jews of the Dispersion as they listened to Christians newly baptised in the Spirit speaking in what to the speakers were unknown tongues.

Scripture also speaks of the tongues of angels. Paul said: 'If I speak with the tongues of men and of angels...' (1 Cor 13:1). Whether our tongues speech ever is angelic we do not know.[4] Nor do we know whether tongues always are, or must always be, living or dead earthly languages. We certainly know that they sometimes are languages in present day use.[5]

Now what is the point and purpose of speaking in tongues? As indicated earlier there are times when normal language can be inadequate or inappropriate and this immediately establishes at least the need for something beyond ordinary speech—and if there is a need there is likely to be a possible means of its fulfilment.

What does Scripture teach? Quite clearly that 'tongues' meet this need in a supernatural way. From 1 Corinthians 14 we learn that a person speaking in tongues does not speak to men but to God, for no man understands. It is emphasised that his mind is barren or unfruitful in the exercise but that nevertheless his spirit is edified. That he does not understand the words he uses becomes even clearer when we read that he is advised to pray that he may interpret, i.e. use another supernatural gift to make his first utterance intelligible to himself and to others. It thus becomes clear that there is a means of communication between man and God which bypasses the understanding but which is spiritually edifying. Without experiencing the phenomenon it is difficult for most people to understand this—but those who do experience it find it significantly true. There can come, for example, a moment of joy in worship when human language under human control seems wholly inadequate. When tongues are used the spirit soars free and expresses itself in a full and uninhibited way. Known language gets out of the way and there is an expression of the spirit which is fully satisfying. Similarly if a person has a heavy burden of prayer he can fix his attention on the matter on hand and let his spirit pray. Tongues are a language of the spirit. This gives great directness and avoids the complication and potential distraction of language under mind control. There is a much closer coming to grips with the issue concerned than is usual in ordinary prayer.

Scripture shows a wide variety of uses of tongues. In a church setting an individual may use them for private edification if he does not have the gift of interpretation or there is no interpreter present. This he will do either silently or in a quiet undertone. He will speak to himself and to God. He may use them publicly but if so they are to be interpreted either by himself or another and there is a limitation on the number of utterances which may be given. There are two views regarding the limitation. Many consider that the limit of two or three relates to the total number of utterances given in one service. I am of the view that the limitation applies to the number of utterances any one individual may give. I feel that this is a truer interpretation of the relevant parts of 1 Corinthians 14 than is the former. (For a more detailed examination of the problem see chapter ten and Appendix three.) Interpretation brings the utterance in tongues into the realm of human understanding and this is important for the edification of the church. When this happens the tongue with the interpretation is equivalent to prophecy, the value of which will be referred to in a later chapter.

In addition to giving utterances the interpretation of which may involve instruction from God to a company (see chapter nine and particularly 1 Corinthians 14:6), tongues are used for prayer—private or public. In the latter case the address will be to God and not from God to man.

Tongues may also be regarded as a kind of half-way house to prophecy and inspired preaching. In normal speaking the person concerned is in control but while thought controls language, language sometimes diverts thought. It is the will of God that preaching should be inspired—the vocal organs and the human mind functioning under His control. Initially it is not easy for an individual to experience this and indeed many never do experience it. It is, however, much easier to come under Divine control in speaking in tongues—where language does not affect concentration and where there is no danger of thoughts wandering through word associations—than it is to be fully controlled in one's own language (as happens in prophecy). When an individual learns how to be controlled in the former realm it becomes easier for him to pass on to full inspiration in his own language.

There is one further use of tongues which has no scriptural precedent but of which we hear from time to time in present day experience. At times anointed preachers have found themselves able to preach directly to foreigners in languages they have never learned and which they do not understand.[6] This is not quite identical with the Acts 2 experience where the people who recognised the tongues used were not being preached to. They were rather onlookers and incidental hearers of their own languages as those baptised spoke to God. A person may sing in tongues and the rule regarding interpretation in public gatherings applies to this too.[7]

Tongues are also seen as a sign—a sign, I take it, of the supernatural Presence of God. 'And these signs shall follow them that believe...they shall speak with new tongues' (Mark 16:17). Speaking in tongues was taken as a sign of the Baptism in the Spirit in the case of Cornelius and his household. In 1 Corinthians 14, tongues are spoken of as a sign to unbelievers.

This gift has become very prominent in recent decades and has been the focus of widespread attention both within the Church and in the secular world.[8] Intermittently through the ages and very strongly from the early twentieth century, sections of the Church and in particular the Pentecostal churches have been familiar with the operation of the gift. From the sixties onwards many believers in the mainline churches have been affected and what is now known as the Charismatic movement has come into being. Most Pentecostals consider that tongues accompany the Baptism in the Spirit. Charismatics recognise tongues and often have the gift but do not generally consider tongues an essential part of the Baptism in the Spirit. Psycholgoists from Jung onwards have been intersted in the phenomenon of glossolalia and their general verdict seems to be that the use of tongues can be beneficial to the persons using them.[9]

I have deliberately kept this chapter short and fairly

uncomplicated—partly because I have already dealt with various aspects of the subject in an earlier book *Reflections on the Baptism in the Holy Spirit*; and again I would emphasise that this chapter should be read in conjunction with the appropriate part of that work.

In another book, *The Clash of Tongues*,[10] the whole subject of tongues, interpretation and prophecy is examined with greater academic rigour.

Notes

[1] This chapter should be read in conjunction with chapter six in *Reflections on the Baptism in the Holy Spirit*. The earlier work deals with some aspects not covered here.

[2] In Fee's view Paul understood tongues to be 'Spirit-inspired utterance... not...out of control,' 'speech essentially unintelligible both to the speaker ([1 Cor] 14:14) and to other hearers' (14:16)...speech directed basically toward God (14:2, 14–15, 28). Fee, *First Epistle to the Corinthians*, p.598.

[3] 'The Spirit who speaks through the prophets is understood to be speaking through "the spirit" of the prophet; when Paul is praying in the Spirit he speaks of "my spirit" praying' (*ibid.*, p.597).

[4] Fee writes: 'That the Corinthians at least... thought of tongues as the language(s) of angels seems highly likely—for two reasons: (1) There is some evidence from Jewish sources that the angels were believed to have their own heavenly language (or dialects) and that by means of the "Spirit" one could speak these dialects.... (2) [One] can make a good deal of sense of the Corinthian view of "spirituality" if they believed that they had already entered into some expression of angelic existence. This would explain their rejection of sexual life and sexual roles (cf. [1 Cor] 7:1–7; 11:2–16) and would also partly explain their denial of a future bodily existence (15:12, 35).... For them the evidence of having "arrived" at such a "spiritual" state would be their speaking the "tongues of angels." Hence the high value placed on this gift' (*ibid.*, pp.630–31).

[5] For a modern example see *Reflections on the Baptism in the Holy Spirit* (chap. 7 and Appendix).

[6] An interesting case of effective preaching (by tribesmen who had no knowledge of the language of the people to whom they preached) is

143

recorded by Bruce Olson in *For This Cross I'll Kill You* (Lakeland, 1977), pp. 147–48). Many of the Yuko tribe were converted as a result.

[7] In addition to individuals singing in tongues, frequently whole companies join in this in our day. It can be very glorious and spiritually uplifting. This particular use of tongues does not seem to have been explicitly indicated in the New Testament but, in my view, should not be discouraged.

[8] Fee indicates: 'The literature here is immense, especially since the outbreak of this phenomenon in the traditional churches in the late 1950's.' See *ibid*., p.597, n.80, for a list of articles from scholarly literature dating from 1960.

[9] See Morton T. Kelsey, *Tongue Speaking* (Crossroad Publishing Company, 1981).

[10] Hugh B. Black, *The Clash of Tongues (1 Corinthians 14)* (forthcoming from New Dawn Books).

9

The Gift of Interpretation

... and to another interpretation of tongues (1 Cor 12:10).

It is evident that the Corinthians were much taken up with the spectacular gift of tongues and were not concerned that what was said should be made meaningful to the whole church. 1 Corinthians 14 is largely devoted to the regulation of the gift of tongues. In Acts 2 we read that 'they all spake in tongues.' There is no suggestion in the text that the tongues which accompanied the Baptism in the Spirit were interpreted or were expected to be interpreted. Nor was there any limitation on the number of persons speaking or on the number of utterances given. It seems probable that in the church at Corinth people found themselves in a similar spiritual atmosphere and were quite happy to go on speaking in tongues endlessly. Paul intervenes to teach them that while a person speaking in tongues edifies himself, the church is not edified unless the tongue is interpreted. The manner of speaking in tongues in the Upper Room was not to be for ever continued. These people, although together, were receiving their personal experiences in the Spirit and were individually in touch with God. In these circumstances it was appropriate for them all to speak in tongues and for them all to speak aloud at the same time. This was not, however, to be the pattern thereafter in normal church gatherings. While there may still be special times of seeking God for the Baptism in the Spirit when a number of people may receive at the same time and all speak in tongues at the same time, this does not mean that normal gatherings of the church should have unlimited speaking aloud in uninterpreted tongues.

It seems as though the Corinthians were much more interested in tongues, even uninterpreted tongues, than they were in prophecy—which Paul regarded as a greater gift. Again and again in 1 Corinthians 14 he argues for the superior merit of the latter gift. He insists that if tongues are publicly used they must be interpreted and he shows that the gift of tongues together with the gift of interpretation is the equivalent of prophecy.

It should be clearly understood that as the gift of tongues is supernatural so is the sister gift of interpretation. This is clearly seen in verse 13, 'Wherefore let him that speaketh in a tongue pray that he may interpret.' If he could have interpreted naturally there would have been no need to pray for the operation of the second gift. As utterances in tongues come by the power of the Spirit, so do the interpretations of the tongues. The question arises: what do interpretations contain? Briefly, everything which prophecies contain, as a close examination of the relevant verses reveals.

Secondly, what is an interpretation? In Pentecostal circles where these gifts are in operation people often ask if it is a translation—and sometimes they notice that an utterance in tongues may be markedly different in length from the interpretation which follows it. Now an interpretation is not necessarily a translation.[1] In ordinary life different people may witness the same event and according to their types and outlooks give different interpretations of it. Types vary and as they vary so do their interpretations. A passage of English literature may be interpreted in two words, or in two thousand. It can be interpreted generally, superficially, or exhaustively. The interpretation will tend to vary according to the character, understanding, ability and insight of the student. So it is in the spiritual realm. A 'tongue' is a spiritual utterance, and the interpretation of the utterance is spiritual. Thus the quality of these may well be affected by the spiritual maturity of the persons through whom they come. This does not make them any the less accurate, nor does it reflect on their Divine origin. In the Bible itself we see differences in type of expression between various writers. For example, John's writings bear features peculiar to himself, and different in type from Mark's. When the former are examined, the same construction of sentence may be seen again and again, and not anywhere else in the New Testament. This in no way impairs the accuracy of the writing or its full inspiration. God pours Himself through men, according to their types. One reason for the great need for Christians to grow deep spiritually is simply that God may be able to use them deeply. More than truth is involved in a message from God to man: power, depth and fulness are all involved and shallowness in a channel can greatly hinder God's purposes. Instead of a deep, spiritually rich utterance being given, a lighter and less penetrating (albeit true and accurate) message may be delivered. Inspiration is not merely a mechanical process, in which the inspired vessel has no part whatever. There is undoubtedly frequently a relationship between the utterance, whether in word or writing, and the channel through whom it comes.

In practice, in interpretation different people find variations in the function of the gift. With some, it is received as a series of pictures; others find thought illumined and directed, and themselves borne along as a ship by the wind. Others again have the impression of reading unfolding lines, as from a page. The means of operating may vary, but the gift is the same, and it can happen that two people in whom the working is different, receive *exactly* the same message (as has happened in the writer's own experience). It should be emphasised that interpretations often are exactly the same—several receiving, and one giving forth.[2] I would emphasise again, however, that interpretation is not necessarily exact translation.

There remains a further point of particular interest.

> For he that speaketh in a tongue speaketh not unto men, but unto God; for no man understandeth; but in the spirit he speaketh mysteries (1 Cor 14:2).

It is apparent from this that the person speaking in tongues is speaking to God[3] and yet very frequently in Pentecostal circles interpretations are manward. How can an interpretation change direction? The answer is quite simple—it does not! When the first utterance is one of praise the interpretation will be one of worship to God. In my own experience some of the most remarkable prayers of praise I have ever heard have been interpretations of tongues. In my earliest days in Pentecostal circles, however, I never heard this. All interpretations were manward and this presented me with a serious problem—for I could see no scriptural basis for the practice. Fortunately before too long I began to understand 1 Corinthians 14:5–6:

> Now I would have you all speak with tongues, but rather that ye should prophesy: and greater is he that prophesieth than he that speaketh with tongues, except he interpret, that the church may receive edifying. But now, brethren, if I come unto you speaking with tongues, what shall I profit you, unless I speak to you

either by way of revelation, or of knowledge, or of prophesying, or of teaching?

The first verse puts the person who speaks in tongues and interprets on a par with the person prophesying. Both edify the church, which is Paul's desired objective. Verse 6 contains the clue to manward interpretation but this is not immediately apparent and one has to go back to the earlier verses of the chapter to see the full significance of the verse. Basically Paul has been saying: prophecy edifies the church —uninterpreted tongues do not. The emphasis is on interpretation. He continues: 'But now, brethren, if I come unto you speaking with tongues [i.e. uninterpreted tongues], what shall I profit you...?' The church was to be edified: 'Hence,' he asks, 'how will you be edified unless I speak to you by way of revelation, or of knowledge, or of prophesying, or of teaching?' In other words, these come through interpretation and all may be contained in interpretation. This is of great significance, and may be easily missed if the dominant line of Paul's argument is not closely followed.

To get the significance more clearly let us recapitulate: Paul puts tongues on one side, and prophecy on the other, and shows the superior merits of the latter. He then shows the comparative uselessness of the former, unless joined to the sister gift of interpretation, in which case the combined gifts are equal to prophecy. Thus he declares that if he comes to the Corinthians merely speaking in tongues he shall not profit them unless he speaks also by way of revelation, or of knowledge, or of prophesying, or of teaching, in which case he would be obeying his own injunction in having the tongue interpreted—these things being contained in interpretation.

That tongues may have a Godward interpretation is clearly seen in verse 2, but verse 6 alone gives Scriptural precedent for the general practice in Pentecostal circles of having manward interpretation of tongues. It is evident from this passage that men were directly addressed in the interpretation. Hence the utterance in tongues must also have been manward although in itself unintelligible. Since verse 6 is the only verse in the Bible which gives scriptural warrant for interpretation being manward, its significance should not be overlooked.

Notes

[1] According to Fee (*First Epistle to the Corinthians*, pp.598–99), 'Although this term could mean something close to "translation," it can also mean "to put into words"; in this context [1 Cor 12:10] it probably means to articulate for the benefit of the community what the tongues-speaker has said. The evidence from 14:5, 13, and 27–28 indicates (a) that this, too, is a "Spirit-inspired" gift of utterance, and (b) that it may be given either to the tongues-speaker or to another.'

[2] In international gatherings two or more may interpret one utterance in tongues, one after the other, for the benefit of the various nationalities present. Hence the accuracy of the interpretations can be tested. This has actually happened, with amazing results. Accuracy has been abundantly demonstrated. Reports of such occurrences may be found from time to time in the publications of the various Pentecostal groups.

[3] Fee has picked up this point. In writing of tongues he says: 'It is speech directed basically toward God ([1 Cor] 14:2, 14–15, 28); one may assume therefore that what is "interpreted" is not speech directed towards others, but the "mysteries" spoken to God.' Fee, *First Epistle to the Corinthians*, p.598.

10

The Gift of Prophecy

...and to another prophecy (1 Cor 12:10).

The gift of prophecy is of tremendous importance. Paul commanded: 'Follow after love, yet desire earnestly spiritual gifts, but rather that ye may prophesy' and again, '...desire earnestly to prophesy' (1 Cor 14:1, 39). This gift he saw as a powerful means of edifying the church of Christ. It was therefore to be greatly sought.

In earlier days when there was widespread opposition to 'Pentecost' within the church, some writers took the view that prophecy was really another name for preaching and attempted to detract from the supernatural nature of the exercise. There are fewer who would maintain this now. The outpouring of the Spirit in recent decades has had a profound effect. Many old arguments in this and related spheres have tended to fade away.

What then is prophecy? It is not merely normal preaching but inspired utterance. It may be, and often is, of a preaching or exhortative nature. That, however, is quite a different thing from putting the matter the other way round, and saying that preaching is prophesying. A study of the Greek and Hebrew words translated 'prophecy' and 'preaching' respectively, makes this abundantly clear. The word used in our chapter heading is *prophēteuō*: to foretell events, speak under inspiration, exercise the prophetic gift, prophesy.[1]

The words translated 'preaching' spring from quite different roots and have quite different meanings:

> *kērussō* to herald—especially divine truth (the gospel), preach, proclaim, publish.
> *kērugma* proclamation, preaching
> *euaggelizō* to announce good news, preach (the gospel)
> *dialegomai* to say thoroughly, to preach unto, to reason (with), to speak.
> *logos* something said.

In none of these cases can there be any possible confusion between prophecy and preaching: a similar distinction is maintained in the Old Testament. The idea that prophecy may be merely forth-telling has no warrant in Scripture; and to read it into it is merely to confuse the issue. Prophecy might be predictive, as in the case of Agabus (Acts 21:10), but it was not necessarily so. On the other hand it was necessarily, and always necessarily, inspired—and this is the vital point.

Professor Peake, of commentary fame, in dealing with prophecy, may be quoted here with benefit:

The prophets were inspired preachers; they spoke as the organs of the Holy Spirit, teaching or exhorting, but also giving new revelations or predicting the future. Paul speaks of them as reading the secrets of men's hearts, which points to a kind of clairvoyant faculty possessed and exercised by them. He appeals to this as one of the convincing signs to the outside world of God's presence in the Church. Apparently they spoke sometimes in an ecstasy. Yet the individual consciousness seems not to have been in abeyance nor the prophet to have lost the power of self-control.

Far removed, surely, from normal preaching![2]

'It is,' Paul said, 'to be earnestly desired.' Why? He who is used in it, is used as the mouthpiece of God. How important such a ministry can be, and is, surely needs no emphasis. It is, for example, possibly more important than the much-coveted gifts of healings, since these minister to the body, whereas prophecy ministers to the spirit.

Lest there be misconception, perhaps a further word should be said about preaching. It is the writer's conviction that while preaching is not necessarily prophecy *all* preaching *ought* to be under unction, and *may and should* reach the fully-inspired level. Preaching is frequently heard which has less than Divine authority and unction and this is commonly accepted. This, however, does not make it Divinely approved. In my view preaching ought always to be God-appointed and God-anointed. Charles G. Finney was most dogmatic on this. To stand as God's representative, as the preacher is held to be, without His commission and anointing was intolerable to him. The gospel, he declared, was better never preached, than preached without the power of the Holy Spirit. Otherwise it might have a hardening and a harmful effect. If this is so we are not really free from our brother's blood until we have taken to him life, in the power of the Spirit. Then does the word become to him a 'savour of life unto life, or death unto death'. What a responsibility devolves upon preachers!

'He that prophesieth speaketh unto men edification and comfort and consolation.' This gives an idea of the content of the gift. Note that in addition to comfort and consolation, edification is included and this may well contain rebuke— since God forever builds on clean ground and sometimes before there is upbuilding there is cleansing. Since tongues with interpretation, as we noted, is equivalent to prophecy it follows that what is contained in interpretation may also be contained in prophecy—i.e. revelation, knowledge and teaching.

In my view there is no essential difference between the two gifts. I have never known a person possess one without the other and indeed if we read a written interpretation without knowing whether there has been a prior utterance in tongues we cannot tell whether it is interpretation or prophecy.

'Why then,' you may ask, 'does God unction one to give a "message" in tongues and another to interpret, when one stage could have been missed out by the use of prophecy?' First, there are people with the gift of tongues who do not have either of the other gifts and God wants to draw them out and use them too. Also, as I have indicated earlier, tongues can act as a half-way house to prophecy and when God is trusted by a person in the first exercise it becomes easier to trust Him in the second and more difficult one. In addition, the use of tongues acts as a sign to unbelievers and can have a profound and beneficial effect on them, whereas they might sometimes fail to recognise the supernatural nature of prophecy.

It should be noted that in the Old Testament, prophecy was very frequently predictive. This continued in the New Testament. Agabus, for example, predicted forthcoming events in the life of Paul. Paul made accurate predictions when, with a ship's crew, he was in peril on the sea. This use of the gift has continued over the centuries with instances too numerous to mention. I will cite one little-known case which relates to my own locality. Sandy Peden, a famous Covenanter leader and preacher, was regarded as a prophet. On one occasion he intimated that a particular house (which, I think, had refused him entrance) would become a ruin and that the highways of the world would pass through it. For years I had known of the prediction. There the ruin stood and seemed likely to stand until the end of time. IBM (the American computer firm) bought the land around the site and built extensively. The main road passed just at the side of the ruin and the ruin was in no way disturbed by the developments. Then in 1984 a new major development took place and a highway passed right through the site. But what of 'highways of the world"? Surely most descriptive of the roads from IBM with its world-wide trade and communications network.

In a local church the blitz on Greenock was predicted publicly in prophecy years before it happened. The town was seen in flames with the people fleeing to the hills. This was accurately fulfilled. When we open ourselves to the gift the predictive element may be expected as God sees fit to give revelation.

There remain two points of considerable difficulty and, since the difficulties apply to both prophecy and tongues, tongues are reintroduced at this point and this section should be read in conjunction with previous comments on page 141.

First, how many may prophesy in one gathering and how many may speak in tongues? What exactly does the Scripture say? In 1 Corinthians 14 we read:

But if all prophesy, and there come in one unbelieving or unlearned, he is reproved by all, he is judged by all; the secrets of his heart are made manifest (v.24).

If any man speaketh in a tongue, let it be by two, or at the most three, and that in turn; and let one interpret (v.27).

And let the prophets speak by two or three, and let the others discern (v.29).

For ye all can prophesy one by one, that all may learn, and all may be comforted; and the spirits of the prophets are subject to the prophets (v.31).

How many utterances in tongues should there be in one service? On the surface it looks like two or at the most three. A close look at the text, however, reveals ambiguity. The limitation may refer to total tongues utterances or equally to the utterances any one individual might give. Had there been no similar reference to numbers in relation to prophecy the matter might have remained obscure. We are told, however, that 'all may prophesy' and again 'let the prophets speak by two or three'. There is obviously a limitation and if the limitation is taken to apply not to the total number of prophecies given in a service, but to the number one individual prophet may give, the matter is resolved. The same reasoning applies to tongues. For fuller treatment of the difficulty see Appendix three.

Secondly, there remains the problem of interpreting verses 22–25:

> Wherefore tongues are for a sign, not to them that believe, but to the unbelieving: but prophesying is for a sign, not to the unbelieving, but to them that believe. If therefore the whole church be assembled together, and all speak with tongues, and there come in men unlearned or unbelieving, will they not say that we are mad? But if all prophesy, and there come in one unbelieving or unlearned, he is reproved by all, he is judged by all; the secrets of his heart are made manifest; and so he will fall down on his face and worship God, declaring that God is among you indeed.

To whom were tongues for a sign and to whom prophecy? Tongues were initially a sign for the unbeliever, but if not properly used—as, for example, if all spoke at once—the unbeliever might consider the company to be mad and in this case the proper function of the gift would completely fail. Prophecy, on the other hand, was a sign to the believer—but so great was this gift that it not only fulfilled this function but also greatly benefited the unbeliever—

although it was not regarded initially as a sign to him. 'See,' Paul might have said, 'how superior this overlooked gift of prophecy is to tongues when these are uninterpreted and the gift abused.' Again, fuller treatment is given in Appendix four.

Some may wonder how verses 24 and 25 are fulfilled in practice. Are people really affected like this when prophecy takes place? And how does it happen? It does in fact frequently happen and it can happen in the following kind of way.

A young man feels a call to the mission field but there are home and financial problems. He thinks God has called him but is not absolutely sure. Perhaps at holiday time he goes into a church which is unknown to him. An unknown prophet rises and just as the young man is thinking of his 'call' the words are used 'and surely it is I the Lord who have called you....' Immediately he thinks of his lack of money for training or going abroad and at once the prophecy seems to follow his thought, 'and take no thought for your life, what ye shall eat, or what ye shall drink; nor yet for your body, what ye shall put on.... but seek ye first the kingdom of God and His righteousness; and all these things shall be added unto you...' 'But Lord,' he thinks, 'what of my mother?' 'I will perfect that which concerneth thee. I will be a Husband to the widow and a Father to the fatherless....' So the prophecy continues until he cannot possibly regard the timing of the promises with that of his own thought as coincidental. He recognises the voice of God. Truly prophecy is a great gift!

One further verse requires comment:

> ...but if there be no interpreter, let him keep silence in the church; and let him speak to himself and to God (v.28).

The meaning of the first part of this verse is straight-forward but raises a fundamental problem. If gifts are gifts of the Spirit are they not necessarily perfect in their operation? Why then is any regulation required? If, for example, no interpreter is present in a gathering how can it be possible for anyone to give an utterance in tongues? The answer really is quite simple. God is perfect. The gift is perfect. But men are fallible. An unction can be on an individual for prayer, for example. The person may, however, be ambitious to prophesy and attempt to do so. This is a very wrong thing to do but it can happen and can cause con-fusion. A person may be deeply through to God and in communication with Him in tongues. He may quite wrongly imagine that he should speak aloud and do so. For this no interpretation will be given. In my view every utterance could be and should be one hundred percent perfect but there are times when the uncrucified flesh creeps in, and sometimes young immature channels make honest mistakes. Thus there is a need for mature spiritual people to judge utterance and maintain a kindly but firm control.

The second part of the verse is also of interest: '...let him speak to himself, and to God.' This may be done either in complete silence—speaking in the heart, or in an undertone which has no disturbing effect on the assembly. In verse 2 we read of an individual speaking to or before God. In my view these verses give warrant for the practice followed in some Pentecostal circles of many people using an undertone of prayer or worship. This should not, however, become so loud that it prevents individuals being heard when they are leading the congregation in prayer, or in prophecy. A moderate undertone is not a contravention of Paul's instruction, but 'let all things be done decently and in order.'

Finally it should be noted that prophecy is to be discerned.

Not all that purports to be prophecy is inspired. For various reasons error can creep in. Sometimes human zeal takes over. Motives can be unworthy. Men may attempt to use prophecy for wrong ends. One of the ways error can creep in is very understandable. A person may have a genuine gift and be used of God from time to time. Individual hearers may greatly benefit and look for God to go on speaking in this way. The prophet begins to assume an important role and people begin to bring him their personal problems, hoping for a 'word from the Lord.' In the Old Testament there was an approved practice of 'enquiring of the Lord,' and sometimes people attempt to do something similar in our day through prophets. Now the human mind, including the mind of the prophet, is seldom if ever completely fallow, and if the prophet begins to ponder a problem at a mind level a solution may very well occur to him. There can be a subtle change from speaking by revelation to speaking from a mind subconsciously affected. If a person is expected to speak and begins to feel that it is his duty to do so, a very real danger of pseudo-prophecy may arise. Mistakes along this line are normally genuine and not deliberate, but the need for discernment must be apparent.

It should also be noted that while an utterance may contain no doctrinal error it is not thereby necessarily true prophecy. With the real gift there is a revelation appropriate to the hour. People with the gift should assess the utterances given.

Again, the reader is referred to *The Clash of Tongues* for more detailed treatment of all the vocal gifts.

Notes

[1] Fee observes that 'Paul's understanding—as well as that of the other NT writers—was thoroughly conditioned by his own history in Judaism. The prophet was a person who spoke to God's people under the inspira-

tion of the Spirit. The "inspired utterance" came by revelation and announced judgment (usually) or salvation. . . . Often the word spoken had a futuristic element, so in that sense they also came to be seen as "predictors"; but that was only one element, and not necessarily the crucial one . . . the evidence in chap. 14 indicates that [prophecy] consisted of spontaneous, Spirit-inspired, intelligible messages, orally delivered in the gathered assembly, intended for the edification or encouragement of the people. And those who prophesied were clearly understood to be "in control" (see 14:29–33)' (*First Epistle to the Corinthians*, p.595). Fee also pointedly indicates that prophecy 'is *not* the delivery of a previously prepared sermon' (*ibid.*).

2   Writing of the whole portion of 1 Corinthians 12:4–11, Fee is very pointed: 'Apart from the traditional Pentecostal movement, the church at large showed very little interest in this paragraph until the outbreak of some of these phenomena both in Roman Catholic and in traditional Protestant circles in the late 1950's. The result has been a considerable body of literature, both scholarly and popular, on the gifts enumerated in vv.8–10 [tongues, interpretation and prophecy]. Most of this literature assumes that such gifts are available to Christians in all ages of the church. Although some have taken a dim view of the phenomena, most have been moderately cautious, suggesting openness to what the Spirit might do, but usually offering correctives or guidelines as well. *However, there has also been a spate of literature whose singular urgency has been to justify the limiting of these gifts to the first-century church* [My italics]. It is fair to say of this literature that its authors have found what they were looking for and have thereby continued to reject such manifestations in the church. *It can also be fairly said that such rejection is not exegetically based, but results in every case from a prior hermeneutical and theological commitment* [My italics].

'Perhaps the greater tragedy for the church is that it should have lost such touch with the Spirit of God in its ongoing life that it should settle for what is only ordinary and thus feel the urgency to justify itself in this way. The hope, of course, lies with v.11, that the one and the same Spirit will do as he pleases, despite the boxes provided for him by those on both sides of this issue' (*ibid.*, pp.599–60).

Again, 'It is of some interest that people who believe so strongly in the Bible as the Word of God should at the same time spend so much energy getting around the plain sense of vv.39–40. Surely there is irony in that. What Paul writes in these chapters he claims to be the command of the Lord; one wonders how he might have applied v.38 to those who completely reject this command [V.38: "But if any man is ignorant, let him be ignorant"]' (*ibid.*, p.713).

11

Other Gifts

The emphasis in this book has been on the nine gifts listed in 1 Corinthians 12. It should not, however, be supposed that these are the only gifts referred to in the New Testament.

A study of the following passages is illuminating:

> And he gave some to be apostles; and some, prophets; and some, evangelists; and some, pastors and teachers (Eph 4:11).

> And God hath set some in the church, first apostles, secondly prophets, thirdly teachers, then miracles, then gifts of healings, helps, governments, divers kind of tongues. Are all apostles? are all prophets? are all teachers? are all workers of miracles? have all gifts of healings? do all speak with tongues? do all interpret? (1 Cor 12:28–30).

> And having gifts differing according to the grace that was given to us, whether prophecy, let us prophesy according to the proportion of our faith; or ministry, let us give ourselves to our ministry; or he that teacheth, to his teaching; or he that exhorteth, to his exhorting: he that giveth, let him do it with liberality; he that ruleth, with diligence; he that sheweth mercy, with cheerfulness (Rom 12:6–8).

It will be noticed that certain of the foregoing lists overlap.

Some seem to contain offices rather than gifts, e.g., apostles, prophets, teachers, evangelists, pastors. These people may be regarded as gifts of the ascended Christ to the Church— but the various categories had their own gifts from the Holy Spirit, e.g., the prophets had prophecy, the teachers had teaching, the evangelist had evangelism, etc. It is important to notice this so that we all may fulfil our proper ministry and recognise what our gifts are and not attempt to be used in spheres to which we are not called. For example, a man may be greatly used in healing. This does not make him a teacher and sometimes when he adopts a wrong role chaos can result. There is a very real gift of teaching and those without it can bore companies dreadfully if they attempt this ministry. Evangelism is a very special gift. A person with it can wonderfully catch the unconverted. Sometimes a teacher who lacks it can give very correct doctrine but reap no harvest in this field. When the gift is in operation the unsaved find it difficult not to respond. Similarly healing can take place remarkably easily when one with the gift is ministering. Faith falls on a company.

In my view the gifts indicated directly or by implication in the New Testament should not necessarily be regarded as the only possible gifts of the Spirit. New movements of the Spirit take place from time to time and as He moves through men there can be new manifestations of His presence and His power. We must not limit Him. Perhaps I could give two illustrations of what I mean. In chapter two I wrote of the gift of knowledge and of the particular call which the Rev. John Hamilton received in Germany. I indicated that he heard the cry of God's people and that God spoke directly to him. 'Again and again,' he says, 'I hear that cry and when I hear it particular things result. Men are set free.' In my view a particular gift comes into operation. There is, of course, the gift of knowledge, but is there not also with it what can only be described as a gift of compassion—not

162

quite the same, I suggest, as love as a fruit of the Spirit—but compassion as a driving force of God?

I have also recently become aware of a particular operation of the Spirit. One of my daughters has increasingly been given insight into satanic (and also Divine) activities. With remarkable accuracy she had been able to keep me informed of things moving behind the scenes. Now in our company there are several people (as I indicated earlier) who are used in exorcism. In the case of one there has also been an awareness of the activities of Satan in a wider dimension. Until now, it never occurred to me that the latter would be a gift in itself quite apart from the power to cast out demons. In the case of my daughter, she has one gift but not the other.

I pray that all readers will know God's blessing and that their appetites will be stimulated to 'desire earnestly spiritual gifts' for the upbuilding of the Body of Christ— that we may be fully equipped for the last great battle before He comes.[1]

Note

[1] You are advised to read the Postscript for background on Corinth as it was in Paul's day. The Appendices which follow may not be of equal interest to all readers. The extract from Norman Grubb in Appendix one and the whole of Appendix two are recommended; the remainder are more specialised and may appeal to students.

General Postscript

It has occurred to me that parts of this book may be more easily understood if they are related to the background against which Paul wrote. Previously a Greek city state, Corinth had been destroyed and a century later refounded as a Roman colony by Julius Caesar. It was very prosperous and became notorious for vice. To 'act like a Corinthian' was another way of saying 'to commit fornication.'[1] Sexual vice was particularly rampant, as indeed it was in any seaport where money was plentiful and prostitutes of both sexes readily available. The population was cosmopolitan, including amongst others Romans, Greeks and Jews. The major part were descended from freed Roman slaves. Paul's Corinth has been described as 'the New York, Los Angeles and Las Vegas of the ancient world.'[2] The young church reflected the society from which its members came. Mainly gentiles, formerly idolators, they had been in the habit of going to temple feasts and immorality had been for many a way of life. There were wide divisions in the church, not only of race—Roman, Greek, Jew—but between freedman and slaves and between rich and poor. Hellenistic influences were strong and Fee could write, 'Although they were the Christian church in Corinth, an inordinate amount of Corinth was yet in them.'[3] Paul had founded the church and, while at Ephesus two years later, had sent them a letter which dealt with problems of immorality and idolatry. They had resented this and had written to him. His reply to this is our First Epistle to the Corinthians. It is the third point of contact Paul had with this church. Tension had risen between Paul and them. He wrote to regulate eleven specific matters—ten of which were behavioural. The influence of Roman and Hellenic thought was very great and many of the abuses with which Paul had to deal arose from those influences. It would seem that with a degree of arrogance many in the church regarded themselves as deeply spiritual. They tended to despise the body, considering that they had reached a plane above body. This led in two opposite directions—one to a permissive attitude to immorality and the other to an asceticism which despised normal marriage relationships. There is some evidence that they regarded speaking in tongues as a mark of super-spirituality. They believed they were sharing the language of angels and assumed that they were thereby already enjoying a heavenly life—this in spite of the gross immorality that was in their midst, about which they were seemingly quite unperturbed. Paul had to bring them down to earth. He dealt with true spirituality and morality, and the proper functioning of the gifts of the Spirit, including tongues. The Corinthians were also particularly interested in knowledge and wisdom and he had to regulate their thinking on this as well, not only in relation to the gifts but in more general terms. While there were divisions amongst them which Paul cited as an evidence of their carnality (shown in their law suits with each other), the main thrust of his letter does not deal so much with divisions between factions within the church as with matters that lay between Paul and the church—e.g. heresies that had risen and were taking them in a Hellenic direction away from both Paul and the gospel he preached. He sought to bring them back to a right foundation and to encourage a proper attitude to his own apostleship which they were evidently questioning. They seem to have had some doubt about this and the degree of his spirituality. They learned! In no apologetic mood Paul goes into battle. His sword is sharp and his teachings have echoed down the years influencing the lives of untold millions. An understanding of the background of this epistle brings home something of the awful pain Paul experienced when his children in Christ turned aside. I have personally sensed this recently as never before. I can in a measure understand what he meant in another context: 'My little children, of whom I am again in travail until Christ be formed in you' (Gal 4:19). Paul was up against strong opposition—but in the end he conquered.

Before his eventual death Paul may have felt that he was going down in defeat. He could mourn, 'All in Asia have turned away from me.' It did seem to be defeat, but we who live in an after age know that he triumphed gloriously. The men who opposed him are long forgotten, or only remembered because they did oppose him. Their views are buried with them; his words live forever. It reminds us of the great apostle's greater Lord. He too died a death of seeming defeat— but rose in power to lead many sons into glory. Seeming tragedy turned to endless triumph. So often it is this way. The darkest hour comes before the dawn, and God's men are sometimes allowed to die before the great light breaks.

Notes

[1] Fee, *First Epistle to the Corinthians*, p.2.
[2] *Ibid.*, p.3.
[3] *Ibid.*, p.4.

The Place of Reason

Extract from 'Commentary on 1 Corinthians 14' (earlier unpublished work by the author).

The human mind has so long, and so wrongly, been enthroned that it is still difficult, even for those who are well aware of the old fallacies, to be quite free from their pernicious influence, and to strike a correct balance in their judgments. It is gradually and increasingly emerging, however, that 'mind' is not the arbiter of action in Man, but is itself subject to deeper underlying forces in personality—its decisions being often conditioned and determined by these. It is interesting in this connection to recall that a number of British professors of philosophy met some years ago, and were astounded to realise that their philosophic views varied according to their psychological types. Where they had felt that their systems of thought had sprung more or less from pure reason, that these were unbiased and the result of calm judgment, it appeared that all along they had been, to some extent at least, duped by deeper, underlying forces in their own personalities—which forces were predisposing them to certain lines of thought. No doubt their views may have been honest, but they were still conditioned views. It is precisely with this deep submerged part in human personality that God deals, and in association with which spiritual gifts function. God desires truth and cleanness in the inner parts, and when Man *is* right, he tends to *think* right. Mind indeed was never meant to be the master, but rather the servant of the soul. Strangely too, or perhaps not so strangely, mind itself reaches its highest attainment and clarity, when it is denied paramount place, and is allowed to function under the control of the Spirit.

Thus in the functioning of the gifts of the Spirit, such as interpretation and prophecy, the mind is, in a sense, passive so far as normal thought processes are concerned, and active only in the sense that it is open Godward; and yet in this passive state its power and perception are infinitely higher than when it is given the primary and active role.

Extract from *An Outline of Psychology* by William McDougall.[2]

The instincts are the prime movers of all human activity; by the conative or impulsive force of some instinct, every train of thought, however cold and passionless it may seem, is borne along towards its end... all the complex intellectual apparatus of the most highly developed mind is but the instrument by which these impulses seek their satisfaction... Take away these instinctive dispositions, with their powerful mechanisms, and the organism would become incapable of activity of any kind; it would be inert and motionless, like a wonderful piece of clockwork whose mainspring had been removed.

Extract from *Guide to Modern Thought* by C. E. M. Joad

[Men] today are fundamentally sceptical of the part played by reasoning in determining our conduct and forming our beliefs. Reason, it is widely suggested, is a mere tool or handmaid of desire. Its function is to secure the ends which we unconsciously set ourselves, by inventing excuses for what we instinctively want to do, and arguments for what we instinctively want to believe....

Psycho-analysts hold, as we have seen, that the forces that dominate our natures are fundamentally instinctive and, therefore, non-rational in character. The unconscious is pictured as a restless sea of instinct and impulse, a sea agitated by gusts of libido, swept by waves of desire, threaded by the currents of urge and drive; and upon these waves and currents consciousness, with all that it contains, bobs helplessly like a cork. Consciousness is represented, in fact, as a sort of by-product of the unconscious. This general conception is exemplified by the attitude current in psycho-analytic literature to reason.

... Of these *natural* forces we know very little, especially since we have succeeded in evolving reason, one of whose main functions is to rationalise them, and so disguise from us their real character. But reason is itself an expression of these instinctive *natural* forces, one of the latest and the weakest. It is a feeble shoot springing from a deep, dim foundation of unconscious strivings, and maintaining a precarious existence as their apologist and their handmaid.

Reason, in fact, is a mere tool of instinct; it is instinct which determines the occasions of its operation and its function is limited to discovering means for satisfying the instincts which employ it. Professor McDougall's theory of instinct points to the same conclusion. 'The instincts,' it will be remembered, are, on this view, 'the prime movers of all human activity... all the complex intellectual apparatus of the most highly developed mind is but the instrument by which these impulses seek their satisfaction.' Reason, in other words, is a mechanism; it is the engine of the person-ality, and instinct is the steam that sets it going. And, since reason can operate only when driven by the impulsive force of instinct, it can proceed only along the path which instinct indicates to the goal which instinct dictates.

Extract from *Christ in Congo Forests* by Norman P. Grubb.[3]

They are fools who belittle such holy experiences, and warn against 'excessive emotionalism'. Such do not even understand the make up of 'Mansoul', still less the ways of the Eternal Lover with His beloved. With sure sense of direction does the inspired Word always point us to the heart, not the mind, as the citadel of Man. It is there that the emotions lie deep-seated, the desires that drive the will, those mysterious fires which burn with the lurid passions of hell, or light up the life with the holy love of heaven, according to the Spirit that dwells in them. The mere mind of man, his views and ideas, his intellectual conceits and opinions, are but straw before the whirlwind in the grip of the real inner man of the heart, when it holds the helm. And revivals reach that inner man, and carry the mind along later as captive in its train. They move the deep springs of being, and all else follows: and they do it in earthquake fashion.

* * *

It might be fair to add that reason if functioning ideally may very well mirror a reality beyond itself and principles governing it may also have a universal validity. My quarrel is not with reason as the handmaid of the soul but with the worship of what is sometimes called reason—but which, in fact, is really a distorted reflection of the true.

Notes

[1] See chap. 1 above.
[2] Culled from C. E. M. Joad, *Guide to Modern Thought* (Faber & Faber Limited, rev. ed. 1948), p.213.
[3] Joad on contemporary psychoanalysts, *ibid.*, pp.219–21.
[4] Norman P. Grubb, *Christ in Congo Forests* (Lutterworth Press, 1945), pp.197–98.

The Compassion of Christ

May I relate another personal experience in connection with the sufferings and care of Christ. From 1968 to 1985 I was Headmaster of a large secondary school, and the day came when drugs began to make their appearance in Scotland. I became aware that they were moving amongst my pupils and that parents were largely ignorant of what was happening. I felt it my duty to warn parents and wrote a very direct letter indicating that some pupils were taking drugs, and naming the kinds of places where drugs were available. As a courtesy, I sent a copy of the letter to my Director of Education, before distributing to parents. Immediately there was consternation! The Director, with the Chairman of the Education Committee, gathered the secondary school Heads for a conference and proposed to issue a common letter to all parents. In my view this letter was so bland that it would have alerted nobody and at the close of the meeting I indicated that I was perfectly willing to send this letter but I wanted to accompany it with my own. This was very unpopular. It is strange how keen both politicians and the police seem to have been to hush up the drug danger in early days. In due course I had a summons from the Director. I will always remember that interview. He pointed to a particular paragraph in my letter and said, 'It is that which is causing the trouble. Could you not take that bit out?' 'That paragraph,' I said, 'is the most important in the letter. It is that paragraph which will really give parents warning.' 'Well,' he said, 'if you put that in you will be crucified.' 'That may well be,' I replied. 'But, you know, in my view a Headmaster has a duty and responsibility to his pupils' parents. It is my bounden duty to give them fair warning of this danger.' My Director was a good man. He looked at me directly and said, 'You are right! Go ahead!'

I sent the letter out and on the following day I had a call from the *Daily Express* who had heard of the matter. Now having had long experience of the Press, and knowing the danger of garbled versions and inaccurate accounts, I preferred them, if printing anything, to print my letter as it stood and I gave them a copy. On the following morning I was on my way to a National Committee meeting in Edinburgh. Looking at newspaper hoardings, what was my horror to read under the heading *Daily Express* the words, 'Drug Abuse: Rector speaks out' and to see an unflattering picture of myself occupying a quarter of the space, as like 'the beast of Belsen' as you may easily imagine! The front page of the paper had a two inch banner headline and my letter was printed in full. I arrived at my meeting and was pursued all day by the Press. I got home in the evening and the pressures increased. The Press wanted more news. This was the first thing of its kind, I suppose, in Scotland. One paper in particular, which was probably annoyed that I had given the *Express* the story while not contacting them, became really objectionable. 'Could you give us the names of the pupils involved?' they asked. 'That,' I said, 'is something no Headmaster worth his salt would ever do.' 'So the truth is that you don't have any names! You are just doing this for publicity!' and so on. I cannot explain this but I felt an overwhelming sense of darkness and oppression coming upon me. It is difficult to rationalise. I had done no more than my duty. I am not a person easily alarmed and yet there came a horrible atmosphere. About midnight I picked up a book by Amy Carmichael and it envisaged in another context something almost identical to what I was passing through. She wrote:

> 'Open thy mouth for the dumb in the cause of all such as are appointed to destruction. Open thy mouth'.... Let any man, anywhere, however detestable all that is involved therein may be to him, obey that command, and uncover some hidden sore of his day and generation, and he will find himself in the pillory. The pillory—it is an uncomfortable word and it is an uncomfortable place... 'For the love of God thou oughtest to suffer all things, labours and sorrows, temptations, vexations, anxieties, necessities, infirmities, wrongs, obloquies, reprehensions, humiliations, confusions, corrections and despites. These things helpeth to virtue, these prove the knight of Christ, these make the heavenly crown.' 'He said not, Thou shalt not be tempested; thou shalt not be travailed; thou shalt not be afflicted: but He said, Thou shalt not be overcome.' And crowds of others, now companions of immortals, spoke their singing words like flutes among the trumpets, and there were living men and women too who were not in the least afraid of pillories, and they came and stood with us there.[2]

I suppose I suddenly realised that I was taking a stand against a tide of the work of Satan and causing all Scotland to be alerted to what was no longer a theoretic but an actual present danger. From the moment the *Express* published the letter the whole country knew. Parents realised that parties could be dangerous things and very probably many a young person was saved. I had not initially been thinking in high spiritual terms. I had simply recognised a duty and sought to fulfil it—but under the surface something very sinister and evil was on the move.

As I read Amy Carmichael I suddenly had a profound spiritual experience. I seemed to go out of the body and I saw Christ on the Cross. He was being attacked by innumerable demons—they were tearing at Him. I cannot easily convey the atmosphere: it was horrific. It is difficult to describe in words: it was a felt thing. It was hell itself let loose. I was made aware that He had moved against organised evil and was suffering the consequences. Suddenly I became aware of His love for those for whom He died—for all men, but in particular, as I saw it in that hour, for the outcasts of humanity—for the alcoholics, the drug addicts, for the very refuse of society. He loved them passionately and desired to embrace them all, and would not be deflected from His purpose, which was their Salvation, in spite of all the force of hell. I have never been quite the same since that hour. Never, now, do I despise any man, although I do not think I had ever been particularly guilty of this. Somehow I came to realise the value of a soul to Christ. He loves all men and He loves them passionately. It is not just a profession of love. It is real love and it is desperately caring. I was asked if I too would go to the cross for others—and specifically if I was prepared to suffer for Him over the drugs business in which I had become involved. The answer was by this point a glad affirmative.

Why do I tell the story? What did I learn? I learned of the love and compassion of Christ which I believe the true prayer warrior must share.

Notes

[1] See chap. 3 above.
[2] *Gold Cord: The Story of a Fellowship* (Christian Literature Crusade, 1974), p.241.

APPENDIX III[1]

1 Corinthians 14

Extracts From Unpublished Commentary By The Author

But if all prophesy, and there come in one unbelieving or unlearned, he is reproved by all, he is judged by all; the secrets of his heart are made manifest; and so he will fall down on his face and worship God, declaring that God is among you indeed (1 Cor 14:24–25).

Here the generally useful nature of prophecy is emphasised. The use of the word 'all,' however, is most difficult to reconcile with verse 29, in which the prophets are instructed to 'prophesy by *two* or *three*.' It almost seems as though the word 'all' is used as an antithesis to the 'all' who speak in tongues in the preceding verse. Here the different reaction is shown and the superior usefulness of prophecy demonstrated. The view that the difficulty may be reconciled by taking the 'two or three' of verse 29, as being the limit for the number prophesying at one and the same time is scarcely tenable, since this would surely lead to disorder, and seems against the spirit of verse 27, where tongues are to be interpreted—and that in turn. Verse 31 puts it altogether out of court for there the prophets are instructed to prophesy 'one by one'. To what then does the limitation of number apply?

> If any man speaketh in a tongue, let it be by two, or at the most three, and that in turn; and let one interpret (v.27).

Paul now gives his ruling as to the use of tongues. Let there be one utterance at a time and let each be interpreted. 'Let one interpret'. The question arises, does 'one' mean someone; the 'one' being impersonal as in the French 'on', and is Paul merely insisting that the utterances be interpreted, or does 'one' mean the numeric 'one'?

The Greek supports the first view, and if this is correct, it allows at least as many interpreters, as there are utterances in one gathering. In present-day practice churches differ; some allow this, while others restrict all the utterances in one service to one interpreter. I favour the first view.

There is yet another divergence in practice in the timing of interpretation. In some cases all the utterance in tongues are given before their interpretations. In others, each interpretation immediately follows the utterance to which it applies. To me, the latter course seems more profitable.

> And let the prophets speak by two or three, and let the others discern (v.29).

The difficulty of the number who may prophesy has been indicated in commenting on verse 24. The matter is again referred to in verse 31, where we read that '*all* may prophesy, *one by one,* that all may learn,' and these verses prevent us from accepting the view that only two or three may prophesy in one service, as appears to be indicated here.

How many then may prophesy? Four possibilities arise:

a) All. Verse 31 reads, 'For ye all can prophesy...'
b) 'Two or three' only. Verse 29 reads, '...let the prophets speak by two or three'.
c) All—but not more than 'two or three' at one time.

d) All—but with one prophet giving not more than two or three utterances.

If verses 24 and 31 alone were to be considered the matter would be perfectly straightforward: for in verse 24 the effect upon the unbeliever of 'all' prophesying is analysed, and the practice seems tacitly approved, and in verse 31 it is distinctly stated that all may prophesy. Verse 29, however, alters the position. Here we read, 'And let the prophets speak by two or three.' Thus if 'two or three' refers to prophets taking part the verses are directly contradictory. If a limitation was not being made, there was no point in mentioning number at all. Again, it cannot be maintained that 'all may prophesy' but no more than two or three *in one service*—for conduct in one service is the very point under discussion, and the church was the place where 'all' were to prophesy.

To evade the difficulty and reconcile these verses some have suggested a third possibility: namely that all may prophesy—but no more than two or three at once. Now, no doubt in the Early Church many did take part in various exercises at one and the same time, but was it not this very kind of thing Paul sought to regulate? The church is to pass from childhood to the mature state. Verse 31 settles the matter beyond doubt. The prophets are to 'prophesy, *one by one*, that all may learn'. This instruction is in harmony with that relating to tongues, which said that they were to be 'in turn'. Thus this argument fails and with it the view that 'two or three' can possibly refer to prophets.

What then can the expression mean? From a study of the Greek alone, a definite ruling cannot be given. The meaning is obscure, and indeed the governing preposition 'by' is not in the original. It is inserted in italics by the Revisers to make the sentence meaningful. The original more exactly reads: 'Let the prophets speak two or three and let the others discern.' On the surface the two or three seems to refer to prophets but it might equally mean 'times' or 'prophecies'. In the light of verses 24 and 31, which definitely make the number who may prophesy unlimited, this verse cannot be regarded as placing a limitation on the number who may prophesy. The only solution which seems possible is that the limitation is on the number of prophecies which one individual may give. This may not at first seem attractive, but the difficulty of rejecting it must be faced. With this interpretation all the difficulties are reconciled. All may prophesy, but each one who does prophesy must do so in turn, and he may not do so more than two or three times in one gathering.

In actual practice in the present day, conduct has been largely conditioned by verses 24 and 31, no limitation being placed on the number of prophecies. The difficulty of verse 29 has been more or less quietly ignored. Hence, so far as practice is concerned, there is nothing so very revolutionary in this view. But the immediate corollary of the view is revolutionary, and yet seems inescapable: if the 'two or three' of verse 29 applies to prophetic utterances given by one individual, and not to the number of individuals giving these utterances, nor to the total number of prophecies, then so must the 'two or at the most three' of verse 27 refer to utterances in tongues by one speaker and not to the number of persons who speak, or to the total number of utterances. The two cases are parallel. The same type of construction is used in each; and what is true of one is true of both. This necessitates a closer re-examination of verse 27. We read, 'If any man speaketh in a tongue, let it be by two, or at the most three, and that in turn; and let one interpret.' 'If any man'—singular—'speaketh in a tongue, let it be by two, or at the most three.' Two or three what— men or tongues? The sense certainly bears the interpretation 'tongues' as well as 'men'. Indeed from the syntax of the sentence this is probably the better rendering. The original may be helpful. It reads more exactly: 'If any man speaketh in a tongue by two or at the most three, and in turn, let one interpret' (the words omitted are in italics in the Revised Version).

There is one serious objection, however. If the 'two or three' refers to utterances by one individual, to what does the 'in turn' refer? In can scarcely refer to these same utterances, since one individual could not in any case speak in two or three tongues at one time, and his utterances would automatically be 'in turn'. From this the 'two or three' would seem more likely to refer to persons who might conceivably be speaking at one and the same time. This argument, however, is not conclusive, nor is the objection fatal. It may well have been that the men who spoke in tongues were to do so in turn and no one was to do so more than three times. This is an equally possible rendering of the sense of the passage.

Secondly the question arises: if the 'two or three' refers to persons how many utterances may these give? There is just no answer. No legislation is laid down. If we make the 'two or three' a limitation of the persons speaking, we cannot then make it a limitation of their utterances in tongues. If it is a limitation of utterances, then we cannot make it a limitation of persons. Surely the only way out of the difficulty is to view it as a limitation, as in prophecy, on the number of utterances by one individual.

In the past there seems to have been much confusion of thought on this subject. Three has generally been regarded as the maximum number of utterances in tongues permissible in one service, whether they come from three individuals or from one. But can this be completely justified? To recapitulate, if the 'three' refers to persons, may these not give an unlimited number of utterances? If it refers to utterances, may not an unlimited number of people give them? We can scarcely have it both ways. The 'two or three' can scarcely be viewed as limiting *both* the speakers and the utterances. It seems more reasonable to view the limitation as one upon the number of utterances by one individual.

Thus from a straightforward analysis of the text of verse 27 a very fair case can be made for more than three utterances in one service. Coupled with the stronger case for more than three utterances in prophecy this is further strengthened. It should be emphasised that the two stand or fall together. The same type of construction is used in each reference and the same arguments are generally applicable.

Now while it has been the general practice in Pentecostal circles to limit the number of utterances in tongues to three while prophecy has been unlimited, it has often been felt that this limitation has had a curbing effect on a large section of the congregation in so far as the use of this gift is concerned. Many have felt unctioned for at least a fourth utterance—which is in itself suggestive—and the above view, which seems to me to be the one which comes nearest to solving all the textual difficulties, would meet this difficulty as well.

However, in the face of established practice it is perhaps scarcely likely that this will be adopted. And it must be admitted that while this may seem the most satisfactory solution, some may feel that too much ambiguity still remains to warrant a change. One would certainly not wish to make of it a 'splitting' question.[2]

Notes

[1] See chaps. 8 and 10 above.

[2] Fee is uncertain as to whether the limitation of number relative to tongues in 1 Corinthians 14 applies to the number who may speak 'at any one service' or 'before there is an interpretation.' In the case of prophecy he is in no doubt that the limitation applies to the number who may speak in sequence and not to the total number of prophecies in one service. See his *First Epistle to the Corinthians*, pp.691–93.

1 Corinthians 14

*Further Extracts From Unpublished Commentary
By The Author*

> In the law it is written, 'By men of strange tongues and by the
> lips of strangers will I speak unto this people; and not even thus
> will they hear me, saith the Lord (v.21).

This commences a section of considerable difficulty.
Indeed many have felt that definite contradiction is contained in the following verses. This, however, is not so, and
a careful study of each verse makes the meaning plain.

First, the quotation is from Isaiah 28:11–12, and the
slight variations in language may be accounted for by the
use of the Septuagint Version.

Second, in what way is 'this people' spoken to by 'men of
strange tongues' and 'the lips of strangers'? Is it directly, in
a way that they understand, through foreigners speaking
their language, as Old Testament commentators probably
thought, or is it in quite another and supernatural way?
That it is the latter, soon emerges.

Finally, 'Not even thus will they hear me...' Despite
such supernatural manifestation the Jews generally would
not accept God's voice. Even in our day the manifestation of
Divine power in the realm of the miraculous does not cause

all to turn to God. When the heart is not right with God, nor prepared to be right, miracle in itself may produce no change. Intellectual conviction is not so important as surrendered will. Thus the manifestation of the Divine Presence, through this supernatural gift of the Spirit, was not destined to turn Israel to God.

> Wherefore tongues are for a sign, not to them that believe, but to the unbelieving: but prophesying is for a sign, not to the unbelieving, but to them that believe (v.22).

The first sentence answers the question of the preceding verse. The people are spoken to by a sign—a supernatural sign. There are various ways in which men may be spoken to, other than by a direct voice. For example, by circumstance, or through inner conviction. In this case they are spoken to by a sign—the sign of tongues, and the speaking is indirect.

The use of this gift, or this sign, in early days, seems to have made a deep impression upon unbelievers—convincing many of the supernatural Presence of God. A similar impression is still often produced in our own day, when the same gift is rightly used. It has often been noticed that the reaction of unbelievers to tongues is markedly different from that of certain prejudiced sections of believers. Young unbiased converts also are remarkably attracted by the gifts of the Spirit and, when properly instructed, generally enter quickly into real Pentecostal experience. It is important too that this should take place before the cooling process (which generally arises soon after conversion) sets in. If a convert is quickly baptised in the Spirit he may maintain the spiritual glow indefinitely.

Now the sign is to the 'unbelieving', not to the 'believing'. Prophecy, however, is a sign to the 'believing', not to the 'unbelieving'. Is there again the suggestion of the same underlying thought in Paul's mind—the superiority of prophecy to tongues in themselves? And in what way is prophecy a sign to the believer? How often one has become aware of the Presence of God in an assembly when some God-anointed prophet has risen to minister. True prophecy is always a sign of the Divine Presence to the believer, and apart from Divine Presence cannot be given. It is, in addition, peculiarly a means whereby God addresses and instructs His own.

> If therefore the whole church be assembled together, and all speak with tongues, and there come in men unlearned or unbelieving, will they not say that ye are mad? (v.23).

Paul now shows what the effect on the unbelievers will be—not through the use—but through the abuse of tongues. Not only will they not be spoken to by them, in the intended way, but they will accuse those speaking of being mad. Notice the phrase: 'if all speak in tongues'; not, 'if some speak in the way which I am about to prescribe.' (There is a danger that in guarding against the abuse, we may destroy the proper function as well. Paul never intended this to happen. His criticism was ever and always of the abuse. Not a breath was raised against the proper use, and he is about to give instruction for this use.) Again and again in modern times, the shattering, God-glorifying effect of 'tongues' upon the unbeliever has been seen when 'tongues' have been properly used.

> But if all prophesy, and there come in one unbelieving or unlearned, he is reproved by all, he is judged by all; the secrets of his heart are made manifest; and so he will fall down on his face and worship God, declaring that God is among you indeed (vv.24–25).

The reaction of the unbeliever to prophecy is dwelt upon at length. This has given rise to the feeling of contradiction.

It has earlier been stated that prophecy is a sign not to the 'unbeliever' but the 'believer', and now its usefulness to the unbeliever is so strongly indicated. There is, however, no contradiction at all. Although the primary function of prophecy is for the believer, Paul shows how it is incidentally beneficial to the unbeliever, whereas tongues, although initially a sign to the unbeliever, when wrongly used defeat their original purpose altogether and serve neither unbeliever nor believer. Thus Paul's main argument is continued. Tongues uninterpreted, or wrongly used, benefit none, not even the unbeliever to whom they are to be a sign; whereas prophecy, although originally a sign to believers and beneficial to them in a direct way, also benefits the unbeliever. Hence the much greater importance of prophecy than uninterpreted tongues in the church gathering. The difficulty consists in confusing the *incidental usefulness* of prophecy to the unbeliever, with its being primarily a *sign* to the believer—two quite different things. The fact that prophecy may apply to the unbeliever does not mean that it is particularly for him, or a sign to him rather than to the believer.

Similar effects to what Paul indicates in this verse are often witnessed today when prophecy is used. The unbeliever is reproved and judged, God's Presence is manifestly known, and often conviction falls. It is marvellous how one utterance can fit so many varied circumstances in so many individuals at one and the same time. Again and again the inner thoughts are written, as it were, upon the wall, and yet generally in such a way that only the individuals concerned are aware of their full significance. Undue embarrassment is avoided but deep searching takes place.

Note

[1] See chap. 10 above.

By the same author

Reflections on the Baptism in the Holy Spirit

The Baptism in the Holy Spirit

- Is it something that happens to us all at conversion, or is it a later and separate experience?
- Should people tarry for it?
- Is it the same as sanctification?
- Do tongues always come with it?
- What about men like Spurgeon and Finney? Did they have this experience?

This book honestly faces many of the problems that the Baptism in the Spirit has raised in the minds of so many in our day. The fact that tens of millions of people now claim to have had this experience, which they describe as similar to what happened to the early disciples on the day of Pentecost, makes the book both topical and relevant.

Published in December 1987, the book has proved very popular and is likely to be used as a textbook on the subject.

£2.25 UK   128pp

By the same author

Reflections on a Song of Love

(A Commentary on 1 Corinthians 13)

First Corinthians Thirteen has a beauty which has enthralled readers through the ages. It highlights Love and reveals attributes of Christ Himself. It has, however, often been used by opponents of pentecostal doctrine—quite wrongly, the author maintains. He raises intriguing questions...

- 'Whether there be tongues, they shall cease'; did this happen with the close of the canon of Scripture?
- Did knowledge cease at the same time? Will knowledge ever cease in this life, and what will replace it in Heaven?
- When Paul became a man he 'put away childish things.' Did this not include tongues?
- Do Christians generally attain the level of Love taught here, and do they display it in their attitudes to each other, as, for example, when these doctrines deeply divide them?

While the main part of this book gives a wonderful description of Christ and the quality of His Love, these controversial issues are not overlooked.

Due for publication in April 1988, this highly original commentary on I Corinthians 13 is likely to attract attention.

£1.25 UK   64pp

By the same author

A Trumpet Call To Women

Is it true that in the Old Testament there were:

    Prophetesses?
    A Woman Judge?
    A Queen (in her own right)?

and in the New Testament:

Prophetesses?	Women Apostles?
Women Teachers?	Women Elders?
Women Evangelists?	Women Deacons?

- What did Paul mean when He taught that in the Church there is neither male or female?
- And was what the Maréchale said true, 'there is no sex in soul'?
- And are all the spiritual functions which are open to men equally open to women?
- Or should women be in a role subject to men?

This is a highly original piece of writing. The author deals in a Biblical way with the question of women ministry. Unlike those who base their case on 'cultural relativism,' Mr Black finds his support in the writings of Paul himself. He produces what to many will be an unexpectedly powerful and persuasive case for the ministry of women.

This is a valuable contribution to the current debate.

Due to be published in April 1988 this thoughtful and original work may be expected to attract wide attention.

£2.50 UK   160pp

By the same author

Battle for the Body

As in battle rival commanders aim for the same strategic points and seek to exploit each other's weaknesses, so in the spiritual war, where the bodies of men are the battlefield, God and Satan aim to secure control of the same vital centres. Each is interested in areas of weakness – Satan that he may enter and destroy – God that He may guard and strengthen. Satan wants the body to be under his control, obeying his commands and ultimately being possessed by him. God wants the same body that it may be wholly His – a channel for His Spirit: holy, strong and pure.

What are the strategic points round which the battle rages?

- The Head
- The Eyes
- The Ears
- The Tongue
- The Shoulders
- The Heart
- The Hands
- The Knees
- The Backbone
- The Feet

You may be surprised at who really controls these parts of our bodies. Examine the evidence as it is revealed in this searching book.

Due for later publication this book has a practical flavour which will appeal to many.

By the same author

The Clash of Tongues

(A Commentary on 1 Corinthians 14)

This work deals not only with the regulation of gifts of the Spirit and their relevance for today but also with some of the deeper principles underlying their use. It raises fundamental questions which are sometimes overlooked:

- How can an individual be edified through speaking something which he cannot understand?
- What is the point of speaking in this way when the hearers do not understand either?
- Is there a spiritual means of communication between the human spirit and God which by-passes the intellect and yields benefit?
- Why did Paul have to make regulations at all? If the gifts are Gifts of the Spirit, how can error creep into their use?
- Do the regulations not clash with the direct unctioning of the Spirit upon an individual?
- Tongues according to verse 2 of 1 Corinthians 14 are Godward. Why then is interpretation in modern times so often manward? Surely if God is addressed in one, He will be addressed in the other. Is there Scriptural justification for the present-day practice?
- Was there a difference between the tongues of Acts 2, which were understood by foreigners, and the 'tongues' of 1 Corinthians 14 which 'no man' understood?

These and other points are dealt with as they arise in the text, and it is hoped that both spiritual and intellectual benefit may be derived from the perusal of the solutions offered.

Due for later publication this book, while of general interest, is expected to appeal particularly to serious students of the New Testament.

BOOK ORDERS

The books advertised on the previous pages are being made available to Christian booksellers throughout the country, but if you have any difficulty in obtaining your supply, you may order directly from New Dawn Books, c/o 27 Denholm Street, Greenock, Scotland PA16 8RH.

·············· ## ORDER FORM ··············

Please send me the books indicated below:

Quantity	Title	Price
	Reflections on the Baptism in the Holy Spirit	£2.25
	Reflections on the Gifts of the Spirit	£2.75
	Reflections on a Song of Love (A commentary on 1 Cor 13)	£1.25
	A Trumpet Call to Women	£2.50
	Consider Him (Twelve Qualities of Christ)	*
	Battle for the Body	*
	The Clash of Tongues (A commentary on 1 Cor 14)	*
	There Shone A Great Light (The Christmas Story)	*

* Prices to be announced

Signature ....

Address ....

....

....

When ordering please send purchase price plus 30p per book to help cover the cost of postage and packaging.

NOTE TO READERS

If you would like to enquire further about issues raised in this book or if you feel that the author could be of help you are invited to write to him at 27 Denholm Street, Greenock or telephone 0475 87432.

It may also be of interest to know that the author is normally involved in five conferences in Scotland each year—New Year, Easter, July, August and October. Friends gather from many parts of Britain. An open invitation is extended to all and particularly to those interested in the Baptism in the Holy Spirit and related themes. Details will be provided on enquiry.